The
Art & Science
of
Storytelling

Learn How to Tell Better Stories
in Conversations,
Business Communication,
Leadership & Brand Building

Quick request

Once complete with the book,
Please provide your honest feedback.

Go to Amazon, type in title of the book.

Click 'Write a Customer Review'

And please provide your thoughts.

Much appreciated!

CONTENTS

Author's Preface

When you think of art, what do you think of? What about science?

Before answering those 2 questions, allow me to give you my perspective.

Art is something that I view as chaos. The less rules, the better. The less rules, the more ability to play.

While with science, I expect the exact opposite. I need rules. Without the rules, there will be havoc. No one wants that!

Therefore, it seems like the 2 are opposite. No way can they play with one another.

False.
The 2 are joined at the hip.

Imagine a person who never saw a coin before. It's your duty to explain to them what it is.

At first glance, you are explaining what the head is.
> o This is the part with the face.

Then you explain what the tail is.
This is the side with a building with a president sitting inside.

The person hearing about the coin is picturing what the coin looks like. In their mind, everything seems separate. One section is for heads, the other section is for tails.

Once you tell them that they are both sides of the same coin, this person looks at you like a fool.

How can they possibly reside on the same plane? They are completely opposite in terms of how you explained them. The guy will no longer view you as a subject matter expert.

Once you show them the coin, it begins to make all the sense in the world.
'Ah… I SEE how a heads and tails can reside on the same domain.'

That is the purpose of this book.

It's one thing to know the theory of storytelling, that's good.

But to go from good to great, you must tell stories. Telling stories is what separates the chumps from the champs.

Just like any field, practice is a must. Storytelling skills are only improved from learning the theory and practicing the fundamentals repeatedly.

I'm a big fan of the fundamentals. However, when I look around other storytelling books and content, I don't see them talking about the fundamentals too much.

Instead, they talk about the derivatives. The plots, settings, characters, and all of that.

'Are you saying those are not the fundamentals?' Correct. The fundamentals are even more simple than that.

Our goal with this book is to unwrap the derivatives and talk about how complexity is built from simplicity.

Let's learn basic division before we try doing long division.

If you are new to the ArmaniTalks brand, let me briefly introduce myself and we will begin.

I am an engineer, Toastmaster, and storyteller. In my early career, I was predominantly in the hard skills fields. I worked as an engineer in the aerospace industry, information technology industry and finance sector.

Later in my career, I started the ArmaniTalks brand which is a media company that distributes short stories on soft skills all around the world.

The 6 skills that my brand covers are the level up mentality (also known as concentration), emotional intelligence, creativity, storytelling, public speaking, and social skills.

From these 6 soft skills, you can master any communication with a human.

My goal with the ArmaniTalks brand is to bring rules to the creative world of communication.

I believe you are caught up with me. If you want to know more, check out armanitalks.com.

Without further ado, lets learn the art & science of storytelling.

What is a Story?

A story is a connection of ideas.
This is the bare fundamental that you need to understand.

A story is not a collection of characters, conflicts, and lessons. Those are the EMERGENT property.

Confusing the emergent property as the source is a recipe for disaster.

Say it with me:
A story is a connection of ideas.

Now the next logical question is:
'What are ideas?'

This is where we are going to have fun.
It all started with a thought.

A thought is a flash that comes in the mind that we bring conscious awareness to.

Picture the mind like a bowl of water.
You are steadily holding this bowl of water.

Heck, I'll give you 100 dollars if you don't move at all! That's how still the bowl of water is.

Suddenly, a little kid comes behind you and starts tickling you. Now the bowl of water is starting to shake. Do you see those waves?

That's how the mind works.

The mind is a medium. Every now and then, we get FLASHES of pictures.

It's been estimated that the average human brain generates ~30,000+ thoughts per day. From those thoughts, we are aware of a few.

The ones that we become aware of often have an emotional charge to it. Therefore, the emotional charge dictates which thoughts we focus on.

At this point, we understand that stories are a connection of ideas.

Now we are understanding that thoughts are flashes in the mind and it's often the emotional charge of the thoughts that will dictate which ones we become aware of.

But are thoughts enough?
No…

We need to provide MEANING.

This is the next question we should ask:
'What the hell is meaning?'

I can talk about this for a while, but I'll keep it simple:

      o Meaning is providing useful value.

'Useful value to who?'
Useful value to anyone.

In later sections, we will talk about how storytelling is a subjective experience. It's a subjective science to the core.

For now, let's learn that our goal is to connect the thoughts in a strategic way to produce an idea.

      o Ideas = an interconnection of thoughts
      o Stories = an interconnection of ideas

You with me so far?
'Yessir.'
Excellent.

The Value of Storytelling

You may be thinking:
'So what? Who cares about stories in the first place?'

As a matter of fact, it's a pretty big deal.
It all started with our ancient ancestors.

Storytelling is not only done with words. It all starts with flashes of pictures in our mind plus the feelings.
That's what cave art is.

Didn't you ever wonder why cave art was a thing? What were our ancient ancestors trying to convey??

They were trying to convey a message.

The discovery of fire was not only used for cooking meat, the discovery of fire was also used for cooking meat, the discovery of fire was also used for ushering in creativity.

With fire, our ancient ancestors were capable of melting items to create their stories...I mean paintings.

They were also able to control time with the use of fire.

In future sections, I'm going to talk about how a true storyteller goes beyond time. Time does not exist to the storyteller. Yes, this book is going to get better the more you read it, that's a guarantee.

With the added control of time, they were able to be creative.

You ever saw a person teaching about wealth?
   o   They say that money buys back your time.

Well, whenever someone has more time,
they go back to their fundamental essence. They want to externalize their internal world:
   o   thoughts and feelings.

Imagine if you had all the money in the world right now. Chances are you will feel more creative than ever.

Although these ancient ancestors didn't have

money, they had fire. Fire gave them back their time and they no longer had to go to sleep when the sun went down.

A lot of the cave art that the ancestors drew were of animals that they were not able to capture. This showed that they were flexing their imagination.

A lot of the cave art was conveying information to future generations.

What's the difference between data and information?
o   Structured data = Information

Information implies meaning while data is hopefully the predecessor to meaning.

Our goal as a storyteller is to create meaning.

This is how the human mind processes the world.

If I just say "dog", "violent", "caffeine pills", then I'm giving you a bunch of data that doesn't mean much.

But if I say:
'Giving caffeine pills to a dog will make them violent.'
Now you have extracted meaning.

I'm not too sure what your job position is, what stage of life you are in, or how many people you deal with.

But you know what I do know?
I know that you deal with people.

When you deal with people, understand they crave meaning. That's where the modern school system messes up.

Growing up, I had a teacher who would randomly give me formulas for her biology exam.

This weird teacher was viewed in the most prestigious light in our school by other teachers. Did her students learn anything?

Her students learned how to memorize random shit.

That's not learning.
A teacher is meant to give **meaning** to their students. My teacher won her awards, but she didn't win the minds & hearts of her students.
If you are dealing with other people, you should aim to give them meaning.

The average mind is thinking so many random thoughts in the day. Allow them to get

information, not data, when they deal with you.
Better yet, allow them to get stories, not only
information when they deal with you.

Information vs Storytelling

'Wait, are you telling me that information and stories are not the same?'
Correct.

Just like:
- o   Structured data = Information
- o   Colored Information = Stories

We are no longer in the Information Age. People are just too slow to catch up. We are now in the *Storytelling Age.*

Don't take my word for it, just look at the data.

It's been estimated that the average human spends roughly 5-7 hours consuming media a day. Blogs, podcasts, radio, tweets, books, etc.

5-7 HOURS!!
That's insane.

What's media?
Media houses colored information aka: stories.

Google gives you information.
Your favorite content creator gives you a story.

The difference?
Personality.

   o   Story = Information + Personality

What is personality?
Are you someone who has a fixed view of
personality or a dynamic one?

If you want to become an elite storyteller, cultivate a dynamic view of personality.

   Allow yourself to evolve from an:
      o Introvert/extrovert to an ambivert.

An ambivert is someone with introverted &
extroverted like tendencies. An ambivert can
adjust at will.

If you are someone who got your Myers Briggs
results a few years ago and have been holding
onto it like it's a life sentence, let go....

A great storyteller is a refined rebel.

o Refined, to not make enemies for no reason.

o Rebel, to not conform for no reason.

As we progress in this journey of learning the art & science of storytelling, our goal is to make one major realization:

o Storytelling is an internal to external transformation.

You may want to grow your brand with more content.

You may want to tell better stories as a leader of your company.

Or you are looking to turn some heads in a business conference that you are going to.

Just know that it all begins with you.

Your personality is the focal point.
From there, we control the minds & hearts of others.

Introspection is the #1 Technology for Storytellers

Storytelling is a subjective science.
What is the main difference between subjective
& objective science?

If it can be objectified, then it is not the subject.
Let's run through a few examples.

Can I observe the mouse that I am clicking?
'Yes.'
Is that the subject?
'No.'

Can I observe my hand?
'Yes.'
Is that the subject?
'No.'

Can I observe my thoughts?
'Yes.'

Is that the subject?
'Uh…no.'

This is where a lot of people will pause.
Heck, it may even spook them out!

We often judge how much of a savage someone is based on what they predominantly identify with. A person who **only** chases sense pleasures is often seen as less civilized. Nothing personal by the way. I am speaking in generalities, of course.

Someone who is well educated says that they are the mind.

o   *'My mind is my #1 tool! I am the mind.'*
This sentence is a contradictory statement.

If the mind is a tool, then it is an object. The subject is anything that **cannot** be objectified. It is the observer.

o   Sophisticated people identify as the mind.
o   Genius storytellers identify as the subject.
Here's a mental hack for introspecting. Say:
"I have a mind & body."

Feel that?
'Uh... yea, I do. What happened?'
You have officially *objectified* the mind and body.

When you have objectified BOTH the mind and body, now you can learn the subjective science.

A storyteller creates meaning out of human experiences. The formula for human experience is:
  o Experience = Subject + Objects

The objects that I am referring to in the line above are the mind & body. Once these 2 are objectified, it becomes much easier to introspect.

'Hey, Armani.'
Yea?
'May be a dumb question, but what exactly is introspecting?'
  o Introspecting = Dwelling + Intent

Have you ever had that moment when you were going from thought to thought without any purpose?
'Yeah.'
That's dwelling.

Dwelling with intent is when we are trying to solve a problem.

Let's say you are someone who gets angry very fast.

The introspection formula will be:
'I have a mind and body.'

This objectifies the mind and body and allows you to identify as the subject.

Then you say:
'I want to know why I have anger issues.'

Intent has been assigned.

This is introspection done the right way.

Eventually, this will become an autopilot act for you. As we are getting started, that's when we are learning the art of objectifying ourselves in a systematic way.

Anything great requires practice.
You may want to take a quick second to try this out.

Follow traumas.
Is there a trauma you've been holding onto?

If so, objectify yourself, and introspect on how to solve that trauma if possible.

Viewing Humans as Computers

There are certain mental models that guide us in life. When you break it down, everything comes down to models.

'Even in engineering?'
Especially in engineering.

When I was in the College of Engineering, a bunch bunch of my professors would give me text-books and tell me to study it.
As I studied it, I saw many different models and formulas. Formulas for voltage, power, resistance and much more.

'What exactly is a formula?'
It's a close approximation that allows us to make meaningful choices and create further useful value.

But the closer you get to the core of a field, the more it feels like it is disappearing!

Formulas help because when a subject is too intangible, the mind can never understand it. That's why we use formulas. To guide the mind into understanding the material.

'What's your formula or mental model for story-telling?'
View humans as computers.

What coding is for computers, stories are for humans.

Technical people often have a tough time learning about psychology because it's too ambiguous.

So, learn about information systems instead, Aka: computers.
I want to dumb it down for you a lot.
A computer processes information.

A computer is broken down into:
- o   Input
- o   Process
- o   Storage
- o   Output

You with me so far?
Okay, let's go more detailed.

Input means how you take in information. Right now, I am writing this book on a Word document. So glamorous!

The computer is **inputting** the knowledge I am giving it through the keyboard buttons.

The next one is **process.**
Processing is when I hit save. When I hit save, there are certain protocols which are activated to save the Word document.

From there? **Storage.**
Storing is saving the document on my computer. I'd be pissed if I worked hard on creating this document for it to only disappear.

Finally, I doubt I'll get through this book in one sitting. So, when I click on the saved document in the future, the computer **outputs** the document on the computer screen.

This is a rough understanding of how information systems work. But I'd be remiss to forget telecommunications.

Let's add one more to the list:
o   Input
o   Process
o   Storage

o   Output

The 5th mighty one is:

o   Telecommunications

Telecommunications allow computers to talk to one another, that's the internet. This is how I'm going to send the final Word document to Amazon after editing.

At this stage, you may be thinking, has this guy gone crazy?? He is supposed to be talking about storytelling. Instead, he's going on a long spiel about computers.

Not quite, my friend.

I'm setting up the analogies. Analogies are a storyteller's weapon of choice.
'What are analogies?'
It's a comparison that allows the human to extract meaningful information.

Computers parallel with humans.

Input is when we take in information. Yoù are reading this book by using your eyes to **input** the words.

Process is when you think about the content.

o   Is it resonating?
o   Is it making logical sense?

o   Is Armani some sort of huckster?

Processing happens at rapid rates.

Storage is you leveraging your memory. The meaningful information is stored in your memory banks so you can recall it later.

After you are done reading this book, you **output** the knowledge to your team.

You command a team of 5 people and want to incorporate storytelling into the culture. So, you **communicate,** and speak your stories into existence to teach your team.

Do you see the parallels between a human and a computer?
'By golly, I do!'
Excellent.

These parallels will help us tremendously because we will cut through the noise and go right into the heart of storytelling skills.

Instead of doing a lot of movement and getting nowhere, we will have a target in mind and go exactly where we need to go.

There are multiple ways to build storytelling

skills and express yourself.

I know this dancer who considers himself a story-teller.

Is this accurate?

Yes, it is!

- o   A dancer can be a storyteller.
- o   So can a musician.
- o   So can a painter.

All are expressing their thoughts & feelings in a tangible form.

However, for the sake of simplicity, I am going to assume that **words** are your main delivery method of choice.

Mastery of words leads to linguistics intelligence.

Linguistics intelligence leads to mastery of story-telling.

Linguistics Intelligence

Linguistics intelligence is the mastery of words. How does someone become a master of words?

In the hard skills dominant fields, you'll often hear the acronym: S.T.E.M.

o Science, Technology, Engineering and Mathematics.

In the soft skills fields, the acronym is: R.L.S.W.

o Reading, Listening, Speaking and Writing.

As we practice our storytelling game, we need to master R.L.S.W. Let's break down each letter.

Reading

Reading is a lost art. But ask any great writer, storyteller, and speaker what they do in their spare time, they'll tell you they read a ton.

There are positive ways to make people read and there are negative tactics.

The positive method is to tell them:
'Reading opens doors and will expand your perspective.'

This should be enough to get people to read, right? Unfortunately, not in the real world.

I had a blend of this with a bunch of fear.

One of the first times I took reading seriously was when I heard this speaker in a YouTube video say:
'If you don't read, then you WILL get dementia.'

The way he said it was in such a serious tone, that I believed him.

I didn't look for evidence to see if what he was saying was factually accurate. At that stage, his TONE was my evidence.
That fear caused me to read. Once I was in, I was all in.

I try to read a book a week.

'Geez, that must be tough!'
If that's tough for you, try to at least read a book every other week. Or a book a month.

If you wanted to read a book in a week, here's the gameplan:

1. Divide the book into 5 parts.
2. Give yourself the weekdays to finish each section.
3. If you can't finish it on the weekdays, then give yourself the weekends to wrap up.

That's a clear target that turns reading a book a week from a wish to a practice.

'What do I read?'
Follow your curiosities.

Often, the curiosities will go wherever your child side goes.

As a child, you probably enjoyed reading. Nowadays, you may hate it because you associate the *feeling of work* to reading.

'I used to read fiction. But isn't reading fiction a waste of time for an adult?'
Not at all.

Reading fiction is one of the most effective ways to learn storytelling.

Let me say that again because you may causally brush off this line:
READING FICTION IS ONE OF THE MOST EFFECTIVE WAYS TO LEARN STORYTELL-ING.

Why?
Because reading fiction allows you to see how an epic story unfolds.

I'm not of the philosophy that you need to take a textbook full of notes. Nah, forget that. Just read the book and see which parts you like and which parts you don't like.

This allows you to develop a FEEL for what's good writing vs bad writing.

Read nonfiction too, of course. Just read wherever your body guides you.

As you read, you will understand the signal/noise ratio.
   o   The signal to noise ratio is a formula that is often used with communications systems.

You ever had the moment when you were blasting a song on the radio and were vibing?
Suddenly, the song started to become more staticky because you were leaving the zone of the radio station.

The clear song was the signal, meaningful information. The static was the noise (junk).

Reading allows you to get to the point efficiently

and prioritize the signal over the noise. Readers ramble less.

Listening

Listening is often viewed as a joke nowadays. Very few people really listen.

A great storyteller talks about real world human experiences. Some of the greatest human experiences are born from pain.

Want to know something?
Most people are giving you direct intel to the topics you could be talking about.
Aka: they are whining.

I used to hate when someone would whine around me. Nowadays, I still hate it, but understand its use. People are giving me direct intel to their problems and struggles.

That's how this book was created.

I'd have a bunch people slide into my Armani-Talks Twitter DMs and be like:
  o 'I have nothing to tell stories about.'
  o 'I don't know if I was born a storyteller.'
  o 'Yo, I'm just not a creative person.'

My clients would tell me similar things as well.

I'd listen intently.
What exactly is the problem?

You have so many thoughts every day. You're telling me you can't string some of those thoughts together and create a story? I'm not buying it!!!

That's when I realized that they had endless content. What they lacked was *direction*.

They were like the man in the desert who hadn't drank water in days. The man was looking at the sands with the HOT sun blasting his face with heat.

At any moment, the man thought he was going to die from dehydration. Only if he could get some water…

Dummy, turn around!!

The water is right behind you. It's an endless stream of water that will hydrate you for the rest of your life!!! Just turn around!

This book is to help you stop looking at the sand and turn around to the water.
   o   The water symbolizes endless ideas, inspiration, and content.

This entire book idea came from me listening to

others.

There are 2 types of listening.

Sponge & trampoline.

Sponge is when you are absorbing information. Trampoline is when you absorb the information and amplify.

If you are watching a documentary, then you are doing sponge listening.

If you are talking to the creator of the documentary, then you are doing trampoline listening. This is when you are absorbing information, asking questions, contributing and much more.

Listeners understand the world on a deeper level by seeing what others miss.

Hearing is only physical. Any dummy can hear. It shows that your ears are working, congrats.

Listening is a physical and mental act. It shows that your ears and concentration levels are working.

Listen more and keep boosting your linguistics intelligence.

Speaking

So, reading and listening is how you input information.

Speaking is one of the ways you output information.
'Speaking? That's easy! I speak all the time.'

You don't speak, you either contribute or ramble.

You ever saw one of those people who claim they think? But in reality, they don't think…they mind wander.

'What's the difference?'

Mind wandering is when you hop from thought to thought. While thinking is when you strategically choose thoughts to fulfill a goal.

A lot of people don't really speak. They just aimlessly say a bunch of words. Mid way into their talking points, they see others looking at them in confusion. That's when the "speaker" wonders: *'How the hell did I end up here?'*

In order to speak, you need to have something worth saying. I don't know why more people don't respect the soft skills field.

It's as though they think you just show up & have it all figured out. What other profession can you have that attitude towards without getting laughed out of the building?

Imagine if I said that I wanted to be an NBA player. That's one thing. It's a completely different thing if I said that 'I am an NBA player.'

It's one thing if I'm playing with my friends at the park. It's another thing to say that I'm a professional who gets paid.

Likewise, with speaking, we need to work with intent. To work with intent, we need to practice.

There are multiple ways to practice speaking:
   o   Start a podcast, YouTube channel, join a Toastmasters, give talks at events etc.

There needs to be at least 1 domain in our lives when we speak with purpose.

For me, I have the ArmaniTalks YouTube channel and the ArmaniTalks podcast.

Both these platforms allow me to speak in depth about strategies, tips and tricks that relate to soft skills.

Others view it as me creating content.

I view it as me taking my speaking skills to the gym.

How bad do you want to master storytelling? How bad are you willing to learn the art and science of this coveted field?

If you really want to learn it, then you need to apply it.

We are not in the game of reading and sitting on our butts.

We are in the game of learning and applying like a superstar. That's real speaking.

Writing

The last thing on the linguistics intelligence formula is writing.

Writing is so underrated that it makes me mad! I would know because I was one of the people who didn't take writing seriously.

My storytelling journey got started when I was working my way up Toastmasters.

I loved the different options for presenting. The options were:

o   Planned speaking.
o   Planned evaluations.
o   Impromptu speaking.

Impromptu speaking is what got me hooked. I loved the idea of being given random topics and creating a talk out of nothing.

This caused me to respect speaking a lot. For some reason, my mind defaulted into viewing writers as lazy.

'Why would I possibly write? I'm speaking. I'm over here creating speeches out of nothing, using my palms, eyes, voice and so much more. Why would I trade that in to sit on my ass and type?'

I think me never using index cards further fueled my disgust towards writing. I was the best man at a wedding once and I saw a bunch of the other speakers reading directly off their cards.

My subconscious mind was associating a negative stigma to the act of writing.

It would take *years* for me to unlearn this junk.

In June 2018, I created the ArmaniTalks Twitter page and made the intent to write tweets of my journey in Toastmasters.

'Did you notice anything?'
Yes, I noticed that the more I wrote tweets, the easier it became for me to speak.

A tweet is simply an idea.
The ideas eventually interconnected and gave me endless topics to speak about.

I was amazed.

Writing allows you to FREEZE your thoughts. When you freeze your thoughts, you objectify yourself even more and become a master of the subjective science known as storytelling.

Let's do a quick refresher, the formula for human experience is:
   o   Experience = Subject + Objects

Objects at the most personal level are our thoughts and body. Well, writing allows you to make direct eye contact with those thoughts.

Master the Art of Words

Linguistics intelligence is simply the vehicle. It's like a car.
The car needs direction.
How do we build direction? Without direction, the storyteller does not progress forward.

Creating Direction
& Pursuing Purpose

The average storyteller is going to read the last section and be like:
'I don't need to consume any more of this book. I have what I need. My goal is to build linguistics intelligence.'

The great storyteller understands that:
'Yes, I need to improve linguistics intelligence. But I can't improve it without direction.'

The great storyteller understands something important about the human mind:
o   **Purpose gives direction.**

Imagine there are 2 brothers, Jacob and Johnny.

Jacob wants to improve his linguistics intelligence to become a master with words.

So, he reads random books, listens to random people, writes about random content pieces, and speaks about random topics.

While Johnny also wants to become a master with words. However, he realizes that to become a master with words, he needs **some** kind of purpose.

His purpose is to be a top tier leader in his company.

For most of Johnny's life, he was a worker who worked behind the scenes.

After 15 years of proving himself, he has finally been given a team. To make sure he doesn't embarrass himself, his goal is to master leadership skills.

For Johnny to create direction, he needs to:
   1.   Know where he is.
   2.   Know where he is going.

Our goal is not to be super specific and detailed. Instead, we want to be general.
   1.   Where is he?
   o   Johnny is a bad leader.
   2.   Where is he going?

o   Johnny wants to be a great leader.

Boom!!! Direction is created.

When Johnny consumes content, he is not wasting his time. Instead, he is reading books that will boost his leadership skills, connecting with past leaders, writing and speaking about content that improves his leadership skills.

At the end of 7 months, who do you think improves their linguistics intelligence more? Jacob or Johnny?
'Uh... Johnny?'
Why?
'Because he had purpose while Jacob didn't.'
That's correct.

It's like me giving you a book with a bunch of random chapters. Would it mean much to you?
'No, it will not.'
Why not?
'Because the book is random.'
Correct.

So, I give you the digital version of the book and say you can do whatever you want to it.

If you're like any curious person, you'll find a way to rearrange the chapters to create meaning out of it. It's impossible to create the meaning without a semblance of a theme.

Understand this... yes, we want to improve our linguistics intelligence. But we need to make sure that we aren't losing sight of the bigger picture.

Create some sort of direction for yourself.

You know this better than me. Why are you reading this book?

Do you want to tell better stories in conversations?
In business?
In life....?

Why?

For me, I knew that I had a lot of stories to tell. I am confident but humble at the same time.

Confident enough to know that I have content worth sharing. Humble enough to know that I don't know diddly squat compared to what I'm supposed to know.

This dynamic allowed me to cultivate desire in learning the storytelling field.
1. I am a mediocre storyteller.
2. I want to become a flawless storyteller.

Is 'flawless' too grand of a target to set for the mind?

Yes & no.

Sure, flawless may not logically be possible. However, in the domain of storytelling, logic is just a means to an end. If I set the goal to become a 'flawless storyteller' I engage what I call a general goal.

General goals don't get much love in our culture! Heck, you can say that general goals often get laughed at.

'You didn't hear? To be terrific, you need to get specific.'

A person with a general goal is often viewed as lazy or as someone who is clueless.

That may work in hard skills dominant fields, but in a field like storytelling, general goals engage **emotion.**

When there is emotion in the goal, the mind takes notice of it. The mind is like:
'Flawless, you say? Let's go for it.'

Now any content that I consume is being

perceived in the context of becoming a flawless storyteller. I can learn from the world at this point.

This is how I create direction and improve my linguistics intelligence along the way.

Create your direction. With direction, the story-telling brain becomes activated.

Fake News:
Content vs Context

Let's take a break from the art and science of storytelling to understand a reason why 'fake news' is becoming a popular phrase nowadays.

It's beyond political.

It ties back to the fundamental nature of storytelling.

If you think propaganda is something new, then buddy, I have some history books to show you.

From those history books I share, how many of its material is set out to fit under a certain agenda?

The whole pandemic of fake news comes down to the idea of content vs context.

Average minds do not know the difference. They'll say the phrase 'context' a bunch. However, they don't understand its true meaning.

Not being able to distinguish content from context leads to brainwashing.

Brainwashing is a story that is believed, whether the story is true or not.

'What is the difference between content and context?"
Content is visible while context is invisible.

Content includes the words, passages, and paragraphs. Context represents the theme.

There was this one time I had a dream...or you can call it a nightmare.

There was a guy who was stealing something from my car. I left my phone in my car as I went to the grocery shop.

As I came out of the grocery shop, I see this guy successfully breaking through my window and is on the verge of stealing my phone.

That's when I snapped.
I hate thieves.

I go up to the person and start smashing his face. Punching him till he is black and blue, literally.

As I'm beating him up, that's when nearby people come and see me attacking him. They decide to record me. The recorded video goes viral on Worldstar.

I start getting flooded with messages from friends, family members and coworkers sending me the video, asking:
'Oh my god Armani, is this you??'

I say, 'yes, but there's a reason WHY I'm being so violent.'

Not only do I hate thieves.
In the context of the dream, someone stole from me earlier that week. Which made this thief stealing from me the 'final straw.'

Are you seeing what I am trying to share?

Focusing only on the content without remotely asking for the context will lead to incomplete information.

That incomplete information will reduce our decision tree of understanding.

The decision tree is the degree of possibilities that our mind has. The smaller the decision tree, the worse off our judgment is.

As a storyteller, we need to be seeking context. The context is important to a storyteller like utensils are important to someone who doesn't like to eat with their hands.

Often, you can prime your mind to look for the context in any occurrences.

A lot of platitudes are just that, platitudes. They aren't final truths which are never meant to be questioned. When a platitude is seen as a law, that's when a lot of incomplete information arises.

I recall this moment when a person in the KFC drive thru was yelling at the cashier. I could hear her yells as I was pulling into the parking lot.

Why was this customer being so mean?

Hasn't she ever heard of the platitude:
'You can always judge someone based on how they treat the service.'

I guess this woman who was yelling at the cashier was just a bad person.

That's when I go past her and enter the drive thru myself.

This is supposed to be a fast-food place. Instead, I end up waiting 30 minutes in the drive thru to finally place my order.

Soon as I get to the area to make my order, the lady greets me with:
'Yea, go.'

Is that how you greet a customer? Whatever, I'm not going to make a fuss.

I ask for my order.
As I'm giving the order, she says:
'Nah. You can't do that.'

I wanted to replace one side item for another item. I do that all the time in the orders. However, she was saying that it was not possible.

At this point, I'm getting agitated. I already waited 30 minutes, and now I am dealing with someone who doesn't know how to do her job.

Did I yell at her? *Nah.*
I go to that fast-food restaurant too much.

But do I understand why the lady in front of me

was yelling at her?
Hell yeah.

Is this the politically correct statement to say?

'Armani, are you really saying you think it's okay to berate a cashier for the service?'
DEPENDS ON THE CONTEXT.

If they are rude first....
Not doing their jobs...
And making a mockery out of the fast-food title...

Then is it really berating or is it providing feedback? This feedback just happens to be loud.

Notice what's going on here.

Context is not always pretty. As we find the context, it requires a whole bunch of getting our hands dirty & actively seeking out more information.

Any bubba can recite a platitude and leave it at that. That's easy. It requires 0 to minimum critical thinking skills.

Storytellers are born from being a refined rebel. They don't give a shit if something is politically correct or not.

If you're a man, allow the idea to be the king and yourself to be the prince.

If you're a woman, allow the idea to be the queen and yourself to be the princess.

Keeping the Idea #1

Spotting the context is difficult. This is what separates average storytellers from great storytellers.

Here's the good news though...
Once you can spot the context by putting in the work, that's when it becomes **much** easier to tell stories.

Average storytellers often start off with the content, and hope that a context presents itself. They twist their fingers and pray.

That's not a strategy, that's acting like a dufus.

It's much better to have a general understanding of the theme, context, and purpose of the story first. That's when the content automatically gets created!

The clearer the context, the easier the content just falls out.

It's much better to ask:
'What's the general message I am trying to get someone to understand?'

Versus asking:
'What words do I use?'

Lead with context first and allow content to follow second. This requires us to retrain our mind.

The brain is naturally lazy. It wants to take the path of least resistance. If it's easy, then the brain will opt for that option.

Now you understand why so many people get brainwashed.

However, to spot the context, we need to change our line of thinking.

This is why we want to keep the idea ahead of us.

I had this teacher in 11th grade named Mr. Bart who once pointed at a man getting out of a car and said:

'One day, this man will be the president of the United States of America.'

The man he was pointing at was Barack Obama.

Obama didn't look special. Heck, he looked like the exact opposite of the other presidents. What made Mr. Bart so confident?

Mr. Bart continued with:
'Barack is a phenomenal speaker.'

Well, you know the rest…

Barack ended up becoming the president of the United States.
Mr. Bart was right.

However, where Mr. Bart lost some of my trust was when he called Barack a 'phenomenal speaker.' Was he really that eloquent?

There was this one episode of the David Letterman show where he clipped a recent Obama interview. In that short interview, Obama said 'uh' at least 40 times! Letterman was mocking him by counting each 'uh.'

How could this be??
He was supposed to be a phenomenal speaker.

Overtime, Obama used less filler words. I'm sure his representatives let him know of his gaffe and Obama ended up fixing some of it.

Guess what?
He did not fix **all** of it.
To this day, Obama says fillers words.

What does this prove?

It implies that even some of the greatest communicators have flaws. That's just the nature of the game.

The difference between an average storyteller and a great storyteller is that one embraces flaws while the other detests them.

Can you guess which is which??

Ironically, the great storyteller embraces flaws. They understand it's a part of the game.

The difference between an average storyteller and a great storyteller is that one embraces flaws while the other detests them.

Can you guess which is which??

Ironically, the great storyteller embraces flaws.

They understand it's a part of the game.

Why are they okay with embracing the flaws?
It's because they keep the IDEA first.

Whatever the idea is, keep it ahead of your identity.

There's a little mental hack I learned to make this easier. This is completely optional by the way.
   •   Have an alternate name.

My name is Arman.
However, I go by Armani too.

Arman is my birth name, and Armani was my nickname growing up.

When my peers would call me Armani growing up, I didn't take any offense to it. Heck, I was often the first person to tell them to call me that.

I noticed when I said my name was 'Arman', they'd forget in a matter of seconds.
When I said my name was 'Armani', they'd never forget.

I noticed this hack was useful in terms of content creation.

When I went by Armani, rather than Arman,

it's as though I was putting my identity **secondary** to something much bigger. And that was the idea.

No need to act like a clown with this hack by the way.
If your name is Ricky, you don't have to become Superman out of nowhere.

Unless it helps.
I'm not judging.

The creative process is much different than the logical process. A lot of what works in the land of creativity will be second guessed in the land of logic.

Don't be so judgmental. Judgement reduces your decision tree while acceptance expands it.

The nickname trick ties into another concept known as the Alter Ego that I bring up in my Level Up Mentality book (currently available on Amazon).

In this section, I talk about how an Alter Ego creates an ideal. An ideal that allows you to get from:
  o   Point A to point B.

Nothing more complicated than that.

I don't mean you need to wear a cape and under-wear, then go to Costco's to force people to put their shopping carts back.

An Alter Ego is simply an ideal that gets you from point A to point B.

The name is powerful.

o   When someone says your name correctly, you feel it.
o   When someone says your name incorrectly, you also feel it.

A lot of great people I know call me 'Armen.' When they try pronouncing 'Arman,' their tongue jams up.

When I say, 'Armani without the I,' they say my name perfectly.

A SLIGHT difference in pronunciation creates feelings in my nervous system.

I write as Armani because it's just a linguistic representation of putting the idea ahead of my identity. This isn't the only way to put the idea ahead of you.

Here are a few other strategies that you can experiment with.

o   Make a logical case for an argument that you vehemently disagree with.

Are you anti-capitalist? Do you think capitalism is evil?

Cool. Make a logical case in **favor** of it.

The ego will fight you. It will be like:
'Those evil capitalists! How can I possibly make a logical case for them?'

I don't know how *you* will do it, but you must. Write an essay making a logical case for it. Whenever your bias creeps in, make yourself aware and check yourself.

If you need to get more information, then get more information. Do further research as to why some people love capitalism.

Let's say you are anti-socialist.
Well, make a logical case for that.

See what those people opposed to you are thinking. Now make a case for them after you get further knowledge.

'What if I don't agree?'
Doesn't matter.

What we are training ourselves to do is to learn how to put the idea in front of our identity.

When we put our identity in front of the idea, we:
o   Reduce our decision tree.
o   Require more willpower to create stories.
o   Feel more performance anxiety.
o   Are heavily biased.

When we put ourselves secondary to the idea, we:
o   Tell stories effortlessly.
o   Are more creative.
o   Feel calm.
o   Are not as biased.

Another way to put the idea in front of our identity is to always be in learning mode.

Always be filling your mind with new information. End each day smarter.

Lifelong learning allows you to realize how many topics you changed *your* mind on.

I've changed my mind many times which allows me to build humility. Trust me, it wasn't always like that.

So, there are 3 options I gave:

- Alternate name.
- Making a case for positions you disagree with.
- Lifelong learning.

You can do all the above, no need to choose one.

The main goal is to put the idea above our tiny little ego.

Only then can we see the context that expands beyond us.

Only Storytelling Exercise You'll Need

![bar separator]

Now's the time to practice telling a story.

I want to give you the easiest storytelling formula out there:

1. Create like no one will see your writing.
2. Edit like everyone will see your writing.

This is how you tell infinite stories about **any** topic out there.

Also, this formula is not only for writing stories, but for speaking as well.

Try it out for yourself.
Here's a prompt that you can play around with:

If you were a Martian who had the power to control all Earthlings for a day, what will you do?

Don't give some politically correct response & don't do much thinking.

I don't want you to sit on your ass and create an outline and all of that. Instead, open a Microsoft document and start creating.

Make the creation process quick. Whatever you think it will take you, divide it by 2.

If you think it will take you 20 minutes to write a 2-page Word document, then give yourself 10 minutes.

We are not focusing on grammar, punctuation, spelling or any of that at the moment.

Instead, we are just focusing on getting the content from:
   o   Our mind -> Reality.
The less time you give yourself, the more you bypass the analytical mind. The more you bypass the analytical mind, the more you engage the emotional picture mind. That's where true creation is born.

Once the time is up, that's when you take a break. 'Why a break?'
The reason we want to take a break is because we are training ourselves into 2 different modes of

thinking:

   o   Creating and editing.

With creating, we are fearless, take risks and lead with emotion.

With editing, we are a scaredy cat, not taking risks and lead with logic.

Therefore, by taking a break, we are training our mind into a new mode of thinking.

'How long should I take the break for?'
That depends on you.

If you are someone who finds it difficult to separate creating & editing, then your breaks need to be longer.

You can write the prompt and resume the next day for editing.

If you are advanced in content creation, then the break can be for just 20 minutes.

I'm going to talk to you like you're a newbie storyteller though.
Wait a day.

(By the way, if you want more writing prompts, check out, *Idea Machine: 333 Creative Writing*

Prompts to Skyrocket your Creativity, on Amazon.)

With editing, our philosophy is different. We are coming back to our writing with a timid attitude.

This is when we assume that everyone is going to see our writing.
- o   Fix up the spelling.
- o   Fix up the grammar.
- o   Fix up the punctuation.

Here's a tip:
There is such a thing as over editing.
With storytelling, our key focus is on the idea, not ourselves.

We don't want to sound so polished that is seems like a robot wrote it. It's better to edit in a way where we are mentally reading our voice.

Do we hear our voice?
That's a great sign.

This storytelling exercise will require practice.
It's only a 2-step formula, but the possibilities are limitless.

You can use it to write blogs, books, tweets, emails, create speeches, YouTube talks, podcasts and much more.

'Are there certain types of topics I should tell stories about?'
o   Write about things you know very well.
o   Write about things you want to know very well.

This all ties back to creating a direction. Linguistics intelligence is a vehicle, but we need some direction. A true storyteller continues to pursue purpose.

From the process of pursuing purpose, they have infinite content material.

That's when they have a wide database of knowledge that allows them to keep leveling up & sharing their ideas.

Measure success on how little you use the backspace button when creating. The less you use the backspace button, the more you are training your mind to become fearless.

The reason we want to be fast with creating is because we want to move out of our own way.

As you are doing the 2-step formula of:
1.   Create like no one will see it.

2. Edit like everyone will see it.

Here's a problem that you will face (guaranteed)…

As you are fiercely typing away, your ego will continue to say:
'What you are writing doesn't make any sense! It's pure gibberish. Quit this nonsense already!!!'

Expect this narrative to come alive in your mind so you can easily shut it down and continue.

I **guarantee** when you come back to your writing during your editing section, the 'gibberish' will make WAY more sense than you expected it to.

Plus, you will also begin surprising yourself.

There will be plenty of moments when you are like:
'Wow, did I really say that? No way! That's a stunning insight.'

The creation process is the hardest part because it requires the most guts.

Not to say that editing is not hard as well. However, editing is easier to implement. Anything that can be outsourced can be seen as the easier one.

Creating the actual story (a good one at that) is something we should never think about outsourcing.

During creating, you'll develop faith & systems thinking.

Sometimes, you'll say something that you don't know how it will connect later. But it does connect.

A storyteller understands a minor detail from chapter 3 can turn into the major plot twist for chapter 31.

Strive For Unique Ideas

One of the platitudes I hate the most is:
'There is no such thing as a new idea.'

There are plenty of respectable people I've seen parroting this platitude as if they are doing the world a favor.

Another quote I hate just as much is:
'Great artists steal.'

I'm not naïve, I get what this quote is trying to say. It's saying that in the initial stages, you don't have a storytelling voice. So, copy your favorite artists, and then over time, add your personality into the mix.

I think both philosophies are flawed and will ensure that you never reach your potential.

For the first platitude, *there is no such thing as a new idea*, I have the exact opposite philosophy.

I think all ideas are new when you look at it correctly.

Let's say I am someone who hates business. I think business is a waste of time.

However, one day, as I am about to reach the pinnacle of my corporate career, I suddenly get fired. My manager decides that my position is no longer needed.

I try to apply for other positions but am unable to land a job due to the job climate.

That's when I decide to give this business thing a shot. I get a course on building a Shopify store, implement the teachings & spend 3-4 years on it.

Overtime, I build a business that dwarfs my old school job's income.

Contrast this with another fellow named Johannes.

Johannes loves his corporate job, but his father gets very sick one day. It was Johannes's father's dream to pass his shoe business down to his only son.

Johannes being a good son understands the work his dad put in and decides to quit his corporate job and help with the shoe business.

That's when he learns the ins and outs of business. Eventually, his business is dwarfing what his old school job made.

Both Johannes and I reached the insight:
    o   Business is not a scam and has the capability of out earning a 9-5 job.

The people who say there is no such thing as a new idea will look at that insight and be like 'see, I told you!! Same exact idea. No such thing as a new idea!! Hehe.'

That's why they will remain subpar.

The genius storyteller is like:
'The final insight is of some interest to me, but it isn't the entire interest. Instead, I'm more curious about **how** you reached that insight in the first place.'

THAT'S WHERE THE REAL STORY BEGINS.

That's where my tone & delivery will be much different than Johannes.

If I got fired from my 9-5 job, then I may have a bitter attitude towards the corporate route. I may say that the corporate route is just as risky, if not more, than the business route because you have less control.

While Johannes does not have the same distaste towards his corporate job. His corporate job was serving him well. Heck, they said he could return if he couldn't make the business work.

In the self-improvement world:
  o   The process is the reward.
In the storytelling world:
  o   The journey is the story.

All ideas are unique when we become journey focused.

You need to become intellectually fearless to discover these ideas.

As for the other quote, great artists steal, that's false.

Plagiarist's steal. Great artists are inspired by life and takes what works for them & discards what doesn't. Simple.

In the beginning stage, I believe an artist shouldn't be stealing, they should be creating even more.

Tell even more stories.
'Do I still consume other content while I'm creating stories?'

Yes. Because the more we keep you as the focal point, the more we can see which styles work for you and which don't.

For me, I love simple writers.

Whenever I see a writer who also writes with simplicity, it further builds my appreciation towards simplicity.

The strategy is to create a lot, start off bumpy, see what you like and don't like from other creators versus going in with the intent to steal and hope that your personality spills in.

Ride the bike without the training wheels from the very beginning.

'Won't we fall a lot?'
Yea, but who cares?

We build more battle scars. The battle scars fuel our creativity for the future.

Advanced storytellers constantly cringe at their past work. The more they cringe at their past work, the more they strengthen their storytelling muscle.

Just like an athlete consumes their film back to watch for the plays they got right and wrong, great storytellers consume their content back to see what they got right and what they can evolve on.

That's the nature of the game. Bottom line? There is such a thing as new ideas.

Strive for new ideas.

That's what makes storytelling an adventure. What a bleak narrative is it to say that there is nothing new out there?

Boring.

Become fantastic by becoming an explorer. Become an explorer by becoming fearless.

Unleash Systems Thinking

What is a system?
Different fields use this phrase in a variety of ways. Can we zone our focus to the first order principles?

I believe so.

A system is composed of:
  o   Creator
  o   Parts
  o   Processes

All stories are systems.
'I thought systems were machines?'
Let's analyze that statement real quick, because that's what the mind often thinks like.

What is a machine?
'A collection of parts that does something useful.'

What decides how the parts will be assembled?
'An idea?'
Correct.

The idea determine which parts will be used and how they will be intertwined. This leads to the machine.

A story is a machine.

o   The creator is the storyteller.
o   The parts are the words, keyboard, mouse etc.
o   The process is how the creator uses those parts to bring the narrative to life.

ALL SYSTEMS HAVE A PURPOSE.

This book is a system.
o   The creator is me.
o   The parts include Amazon KDP, my computer, Microsoft document etc.   `
o   The process is how I interconnected the sections and chapters to create the book.

The purpose of the book is to create great storytellers.

How can you unleash systems thinking?
By becoming an artistic engineer.

o   An artist focuses on the whole.
o   An engineer focuses on the parts.

Let's use our palm as an example.

What do you see first?
'I see a palm.'
You don't see a thumb, index finger, middle finger, ring finger and pinky, first?
'No, I see those second. I see the palm first.'
Yes, me too.

A systems thinker focuses on the big picture first then narrows down to the details. It's like ordering a burger from McDonalds.

I doubt you go to the cashier and are like:
'I will get sesame seeds, buns, patties, mustard, pickles, cheese, blah, blah, blah.'

That's unnecessary.

Say, 'I will get a cheeseburger' and then customize after the general understanding has been acknowledged.

As common sense as this may seem, many storytellers go straight for the little details without focusing on the big picture first.

They strive for the content but have little idea of the context.

This is why storytelling is very difficult for them. They are going against the grain of how the mind works.

The mind likes to focus on the big system first and then goes smaller into the details later.

Look around your living facility. You'll see words are designed for you to acknowledge the big picture first.

Example:
You open your door, what do you enter?
'My living room.'

See? You didn't say a room with a carpet, TV, lights, and all of that.
You just said, *living room.*

Living room is a system that's composed of parts. Those parts are organized in a particular way to give you a pleasant home experience.

Same thing with when you have to go to the bathroom, what do you say?
'I need to go to the bathroom.'

Bathroom is also a system.
It's composed of multiple parts that are organized in multiple ways to create useful value.

Just because storytelling is in the domain of ideas does NOT mean it's not a system. You could argue that without stories, physical systems would NOT exist.

This is where analogies are king.

o   Physical property is made from glass, cement, and wood.
o   Digital property is made from stories, concepts, and ideas.

Systems thinking is something we train our mind into with stories & focusing on the big idea first.

Typically, this is where brainstorming helps.

'How does someone brainstorm to get their mind thinking differently?'
Multiple ways.

You know what?? Let me give you a full section on brainstorming.

Brainstorming

---

o   In social skills, mumbling is awful.
o   With storytelling, mumbling is a coveted skill.

'Mumbling is a coveted skill? What the hell are you talking about?'
Yes.
o   Mumbling prevents you from committing.

Let's say you don't have a notepad, pencil, or anything like that. I tell you to give a talk on a field that you're very knowledgeable on.

Your goal is to talk about poodles.
'How did you know I knew about poodles??'
Eh, just a lucky guess, lol.

Okay, so give me a talk about poodles. Teach me something so I can appreciate this animal as

That's when you are going to recall information about poodles from your memory. Play around with what works and what doesn't. Mumble, but don't commit.

'Poodles are good because they cu...te..'
'Cat & poodles are eh...'
'Poodles are low maintena..'

There is a bunch of chaos. Behind this chaos is you hopping from node to node.

A node is another word for a component. We are not connecting the nodes yet; we are just identifying the nodes.

Eventually, we have 3 nodes after our little mumbling spree.

o   Poodles are cute.
o   Poodles are low maintenance.
o   Poodles will help you pick up woman if you're single.

The question is, how do you link these 3 nodes together?

A storyteller:
1.   Creates the nodes.
2.   Links the nodes.

That's brainstorming in a nutshell.

How you link the nodes is completely up to you.

Do you see how the brainstorming through mumbling process happened?

Sample talk from brainstorming:

'Listen man, I know you're a cat person. But let me tell you why poodles are great. Poodles have a bunch of benefits. The first benefit is that they are cute. How cute you ask? Cute enough for you to pick up woman as a single man in New York city. I know you're always taking the subway to save money. That's why poodles are clutch. They are low maintenance & highly affordable.'

This is our string of ideas which gave an understanding of poodles. We didn't make it too complex.

We can absolutely make it more complex and richer if need be. However, at the moment, we are just introducing our mind to systems thinking.

'Do nodes and links always have to be mumbled into existence?'
No, another way to brainstorm is by journaling or drawing.

Create boxes with your ideas and then connect those ideas as you see fit.

A storyteller's mind looks like 1 big web. They see everything in interconnections. The web represents their supreme creativity.

When you see your drawing of the web firsthand, that's when we can hop from node to node.

That's very similar to how the internet works by the way.

For the internet, the message from a particular computer is chopped up into packets. Then the packets are transferred among different routes & different paths to get to the target's computer.

The different nodes are linked in alternate ways to go from point A to point B.

So, how you link your nodes is completely up to you. If you're an advanced storyteller, you will often become very unpredictable. You'll create nodes that very **disparate** from one another, and still find a way to link them together.

Storytelling Exercise: Linking Nodes

Here are 5 different nodes:
1. The sheep is purple.
2. An asteroid is hitting Earth on Friday.
3. Computers can walk.
4. What is the meaning of life?
5. Logic vs emotion.

Find a way to intertwine these 5 different nodes to create a talk.

Have fun.

Nodes & Links

Earlier, I said systems had:
o   Creator
o   Parts
o   Processes

Another way to look at systems is through:
o   Nodes and links

Either mindset works.

'Why the different definitions?'
They aren't different. More so, they are different
angles of looking at the same thing.

It's like the game of basketball. The game has a
section for offense and another section for
defense.

When a player goes from offense to defense, it's 2 different ways of looking at the same game.

As you were attempting to connect the 5 nodes I gave you in the last exercise, I'm sure you can understand how much of a creative exercise it is to link nodes.

What about the creator, process, and parts formula?

The creator was you.
The parts included the 5 nodes and your pencil and paper if you were writing.
The process depends on how you told the story.

Notice the intricacy that is naturally emerging. Do you see why I said it's ridiculous to believe the platitude that 'no idea is unique?'

All ideas are unique.

The more ideas you create, the more you unlock the mindset of a creator.

Storytelling shifts your perception of reality.

Perception is:
   o   Sense impressions + Story

We are getting a bunch of data coming from the external world. Then we have a bunch of neurons which take in the information that is 'important.'

This is often why you'll see 2 different people looking at the same thing, but they are seeing 2 completely different things. It's because their stories of what is important is different.

We focus mainly on the physical because that's measurable. However, the story is what is required for the perception to be complete.

When you get in the habit of creating stories, you start to identify more as the creator, rather than the parts and processes of a system.

When you identify as the creator, that's when you unlock **superset thinking.**

This is the type of thinking which allows you to:
1. See the systems all around in life.
2. See the same creator within all systems.

This gives a new meaning to seeing the unity behind diversity. Plenty of people say that 'all is one.' However, storytelling allows you to experience that on a first-hand basis.

MIND BLOWING!!!!

I was collecting nodes.

I was using that content to see the context of what makes people angry. How real-world emotions manifest suddenly. How certain places lead to more anger than other places. Like places where there were big lines, there was more anger.

I was noticing random little details, not thinking much of it.

Later in the game, I wrote a fiction book, called, *Cobra: A Story on Social Anxiety, People Skills, Leadership & Greatness (currently available on Amazon).*

In the book, there were a few sections where I got the anger emotion of the fast-food workers and cross applied it to my main character.

Hm.
What was going on?

What was going on was that I did a link and node combination!

The same anger that a customer felt in one of the public freakouts was the same anger that the main character Cobra felt when he learned that one of his interns accidentally deleted his code.

This went onto show that when you are absorbing nodes, you never know which content will come in handy.

It may be a tad bit risky for me to say this, but oh well.
   o   **For a storyteller, no content is bad content.**
All content can serve as nodes.

'Even the dangerous ones?'
Yes. Not the politically correct answer, but it's true.

The question is, *what is dangerous content?*
That is subjective.

Think if you were the guardian of someone. What are some content pieces you would not want them watching? Consider that as your perspective of *dangerous*.

I'm sure the typical answers will be:
   o   Reality TV shows.
   o   Political propaganda.
   o   Music videos with curse words.

'Yes, I'd say all those stuff. Are you telling me you can learn storytelling from that?'
Yes.

Once again, I know this isn't the politically correct thing to say. The politically correct things to say is:
'Learn storytelling by watching Netflix & reading fiction books. That's all you need.'

Yes, Netflix and fiction books will help you out tremendously.

But to be a great storyteller, you need to be non-discriminatory towards ANY nodes.

All nodes will come back later to serve you if you are a prolific creator.

Let me give you one more example so it starts to click.

I used to be obsessed with battle rap a few years back. Anytime I was having a good day, I'd watch some battle rap. Whenever I was having a bad day, I'd watch some battle rap. At the time, I had no clue why I was consuming this material, I just was.

Well, there was a battle when one of the rappers showed up drunk.

Not just a bit drunk where he was friendly. Instead, it was enough to throw off the entire atmosphere.

What made it more daunting was that the guy was a 6-foot 5 behemoth. Seeing him that drunk was even more terrifying.

The drunk behavior was enough to ruin the mood of the entire event. Good going!!

A few years later, I had a buddy of mine who was applying to be a lawyer. In law school, you have this end of the semester project where you partici-pate in a mock trial.

You're given a case, witnesses, judge, and all that. My friend invited me to the mock trial along with a few other kids.

Let's call this lawyer buddy, Hari.

Hari was louder than usual. He seemed like he was being very aggressive. To an outsider, it seemed like Hari was just trying to win the case. As a friend who knew him for 8 years, I knew he was drunk.

Suddenly, I saw the similar connections from the mock trial to the battle rap event.

What was unique about this was that Hari was

tiny, where the battle rapper was a giant. This allowed me to scc the entire scenario from a different context.

I saw how much of a role that height played in terms of perceived aggression when someone is drunk. Also, I saw how some people use alcohol to unwind before stressful moments.

    o   For a battle rapper, their battle is a high stakes event.
    o   For a law student, their mock trial is a high stakes event.

Seeing these 2 disparate nodes, link, was mind blowing to me. I used the insights learned from these 2 events to create an email on my Armani-Talks daily newsletter (which you can sign up for on armanitalks.com/newsletter) called, *Addictions*.

The *Addictions* story talks about how difficult it is to overcome an addiction. It's because the person who is trying to overcome it does not only feel mental pain, but they feel physical pain too.

You never know which node will come in handy when creating stories.

How to Create Infinite Content

Let's do a quick recap of a few important points.

o   Storytelling is a connection of ideas.
o   Storytelling is a subjective science.
o   Storytelling is done best when you report back on real world human experiences.
o   Stories are systems that you create.
o   To practice storytelling, create like no one will see it & edit like everyone will see it.

Sound good so far?
'Yes, sounds good.'

Another thing I want you to understand is the concept of practice.

Do you have a definition of practice?
'It's when you just keep repeating something.'

That's a very sloppy definition, my friend. Sloppy definitions lead to sloppy behavior.

If we want to practice storytelling like a superstar athlete, then we need to have a solid definition of practice.

'Alright smart guy, what's your definition?'
   o   Practice is when you rewire your *nervous system.*

Your nervous system is the information processing centers of you as a person.

I don't know about you, but whenever I hear the phrase, nervous system, I think something serious. This increases the stakes of practicing.

To raise the stakes even more, add in a timer.

Something about a timer counting down unleashes a primal side in me.

This is a 2-step combination of practice:
   1.   Rewire your nervous system.
   2.   Leverage a timer.

Practice telling stories about anything that deals with human experiences.

Too many people talk about:
'Finding your niche.'

I think this is subpar advice for content creation. Finding your niche is a great advice for products.

I used to own this stainless-steel tumbler brand. The only problem was that there were multiple people on Amazon who were also selling the same exact product.

My business partner and I needed a way to stick out. So, after some time, we did research on what everyone else was doing. They were all targeting their tumblers to different groups of people.

Some were marketing their tumblers for busy workers who traveled a lot and wanted to keep their coffee warm.

Others were selling to students who needed to keep their water cool as they pulled an all-nighter.

My business partner and I decided to appeal to people who loved hiking. This was the niche that we would target.

Overtime, our tumblers began selling like hotcakes. Guess the *find your niche* advice was great.

Yes, for products.
But for people, it's better to find your theme.

Themes allow you to be an expansive thinker who can easily extract meaning out of content (your experiences).

Allow me to give you 2 examples.

One example is Robert Kiyosaki and his Rich Dad company.

Robert Kiyosaki is the author of the highest selling personal finance book of all time, Rich Dad Poor Dad.

The book outlines the 2 types of financial advice that his 2 'dads' gave him.

One was his biological dad, who was the poor dad. The other one was his rich dad, who was his best friend's father.

The story explains how the 2 different philosophies of the men molded Robert's view of money.

Imagine if Robert Kiyosaki did not have the theme of personal finance for his brand. Then he'd just look at those experiences and see

nothing much. He'd be like:
'I have 2 guys who are randomly giving me advice.'

However, when he put the **theme** of personal finance to his experiences, he was given a new sunglass to reality!

Now, he was able to scope through the fluff to find the **meaningful** information. Imagine how much he can monetize his memories if he searches enough.

Another example is the ArmaniTalks brand.

I've had a wide range of experiences in my life.
  o   Lived in the Eastern and Western sides of the world.
  o   I was in a hard skills dominant field along with a soft skills dominant field.
  o   And worked with different entrepreneurs from all around the world to help them improve their storytelling skills.

The question is, *so what?*
It means nothing if I don't have a theme.

Luckily, the theme of the ArmaniTalks brand is communication skills.

With this theme, I am given a new sunglass to

reality.

With the new sunglass to reality, I can explore my experiences in a new light.

This allows me to find meaning in any experience. Plus, since this is my experience and no one else's, unique content is a byproduct.

For you to create infinite content, you want to ask yourself:
   o   What is the theme of my content?

No need to be super specific.
Being general is the way to go.

Just for a bit more context to help you out, the ArmaniTalks brand started off as a public speaking account.

I would only give public speaking advice and leave it at that. So, you could say that I niched myself in too deep.

Overtime, I noticed there were other tips that I would give. Public speaking was a master class on *social skills*. If you can talk to 50 people with ease, then 4 people were light work.

Overtime, I added in social skills to my content arsenal.

As I added in social skills, I noticed a ton of people were too logical with humans. They didn't understand that humans were emotional creatures first and logical creatures second. I'd know because I used to be too logical for so long.

o   When you expect humans to be logical creatures, you get impatience.
o   When you expect humans to be flawed creatures, you get patience.

Soon enough, another content piece added to my arsenal was emotional *intelligence.*

From there, I added in a few other soft skills. As 1 year had passed, I had the following soft skills:
o   Concentration
o   Public speaking
o   Social skills
o   Emotional intelligence
o   Creativity
o   Storytelling

These 5-6 nodes allowed the theme of 'communication skills' to naturally emerge.

Robert Kiyosaki's content speaks about:
o   Entrepreneurship
o   Accounting
o   Mindset

o   Investing
o   Negotiation
o   Etc.

And the emergent property of all that is the theme of 'personal finance.'

If you have a theme, then you have a new sunglass to reality.

When others see you constantly chugging out content, they wonder:
'How does this person get all these ideas?'

It's because you are mining your experiences.

Mining your Experiences

The best stories are inspired by truth.
You ever heard of Game of Thrones?
'Yes.'
You ever heard of George R.R. Martin?
'Who??'
Fool! His stories are what Game of Thrones is based on.

Anyways, he is a famous fiction author. You would assume that his fiction journey was getting lost in fantasy and making random things up.

False.

He said his fiction writing journey started when he was getting his heart broken as a youngster.

His broken heart caused him to feel a lot of emotions. Those emotions were channeled into a a creative outlet. That creative outlet was fiction. His fiction works were an outlet for **real world** human experiences and emotions.

When you are creating content, one of the smartest things you can do is to use real world experiences to the best of your abilities.

'But Armani, I haven't gone through all emotions and experiences. What if I want to go beyond my comfort zone and talk about characters that have done things that I haven't?'
That's something that is possible.

   o   Since you are always learning, you are collecting nodes from other creations.
   o   Since you are always introspecting, you're clarifying your nodes.

Cross combining your nodes with other nodes leads to the creation of unique content.   ˋ

I have not physically flown in my life, but I do have the human desire to expand beyond my horizon. Guess who has flown?
'Who?'
A bird.

So, I watch documentaries of birds.
Then I cross combine my desire with the physical act of flying to create a new

compelling character.

The name of the game is mining your experiences. Let's give a real-world example so we can understand.

Imagine that there is a dirt hill.
Within this dirt hill are tons of gold.

With me so far?
'Yessir.'

Imagine if I just got the gold out of the hills and wanted to build a business around that. Is that effective?
'Yea, why not?'

Let's be more creative. Sure, a lot of people would just want raw gold, but let's put our entrepreneurial hat on.

'It would be better if we can make gold necklaces, gold earrings and gold bracelets.'
Bingo! We turn the gold into products and sell them to consumers.

1. We extract raw gold.
2. We manufacture the gold into necklaces, earrings, and bracelets.
3. Then we sell to consumers.

Likewise, the same thing happens with storytelling.

Instead of mining gold, we are mining our memories. If you mine your memories correctly, it is equivalent to gold.

Let's say your theme is to make women feel more confident through styling their makeup.

1. Find memories of when you were unconfident and felt confident through makeup.
2. Manufacture a story and put it in the form of tweets, blogs, and videos.
3. Then give it to an end consumer.

Mining your experiences is key.

In the land of storytelling, lead with yourself first and everything else will be derivatives.

The Art of Noticing Things

Learn to create stories about yourself and it will be much easier to tell stories about others.

What beginners do is they rush it.

They want to magically create stories on dragons, demons, and talking lizards. But they can't even tell a compelling story about their day.

Learn to crawl before you're trying to run.

Get rid of the notion that you need to make a grand spectacle to be a storyteller. That's not remotely true.

Instead, start off with the boring.

Jerry Seinfeld is a legendary comedian who is almost a billionaire because he was capable of noticing the little things.

Any dummy can notice 1 thing though.
It takes skill to notice a **series** of things in 1 item.

I'll give you an example.

A wallet. You have one of those?
'Yes.'
Which pocket do you put your wallet in?
'Front right, of course.'
I put it in my back right.
'Are you insane?? Someone can easily pick pocket you! Plus, sitting on your wallet is bad for your spine.'
I know. But for some reason, I can't help it.
'Logically, you know you are wrong. Why not stop?'
Because emotionally, I've conditioned myself to live this way.

A few things.

1.   I noticed different people put their wallets in different spots.
2.   Logically, I know my method is wrong.
3.   Despite logic showing its face, I am allowing emotions to overrule my behavior.

I can notice a lot more things by the way. Such as:
o   How a lot of people don't even have wallets anymore, they have those card clip holders.

o   Whose idea was it to create the wallet in the first place?

o   When the wallet was initially created, where did the inventor put his wallet: Front or back pocket?

o   How come men have wallets and not purses?

This can go on for a long time. It's all about me noticing a series of things.

If I just notice one thing, then I will not flex my creative muscles. The more I notice a series of things, the easier it becomes for me to tell stories.

Creative Exercise: Notice Things

Find a random item in your living facility and noticed 40 things about it.
'40? I can barely notice 4 things about it.'

Aim for 40.

Each time you feel like you are done and not capable of noticing more, you'll find yourself noticing more.

This is yoga for the mind
You're stretching.

Further, further, and further….

Mental Sports: Superstar Athlete

Average storytellers feel inspiration and write stories.
Great storytellers write stories and then feel inspiration.

In the creative fields, it's easy to get lazy. There are many people who make excuses and say that discipline is not needed.

Big mistake.

Because if you cannot systemize your creativity, then you will go insane. It's not a matter of *if*, it's a matter of *when*.

This is why having some sort of practice is clutch.
I loved sports growing up. I played basketball,

football, swam and much more.

The thing I would notice is that superstar athletes had a shelf life. A player would not say that they could play basketball until they were 60 years old.

That's ridiculous! For the most part, they knew their body would not be able to fight father time.

For mental sports, it's entirely different.

We will tell our best stories the more years we add on. That's because now we:
  o   Have more life experience.
  o   Have a portfolio of content that we can draw inspiration from.
  o   Have a solid work ethic (hopefully).

With this perspective, it becomes much easier to create content for life. Still, without work ethic, nothing is possible.

I have a simple writing and speaking schedule I follow every week.

  o   Daily emails.
  o   A YouTube video every Monday, Wednesday, and Friday.
  o   A podcast every Tuesday, Thursday, and

Saturday.

These are acts that I have programmed myself into doing.

This is when deliberate practice comes in.
I start the timer, create, and publish.
Easy peasy lemon squeezy.

However, we are going to make it difficult.
'Why?'
It's because being disciplined with storytelling is a foreign concept.

It's because we are playing a game with the mind. Whenever the mind is involved, respectable people become childish.

'Oh, the mind. It's just the way it is. I can't do anything about it,' they say.
Of course, you can.

Every time you tell a story, you change your perception of yourself. You linguistically rewire your nervous system.

Words allow you to travel across time:
o   Make sense of the *past*.
o   Bring clarity to the *present*.
o   Engineer your path towards the *future*.

These are compelling reasons to tell stories every day.

To cultivate the attitude of a superstar athlete, here are 2 golden rules to follow:

1. 1% improvement is key.
2. Plan for when you're sick.

For 1, it's all about starting small and allowing the snowball to turn into an avalanche.

You don't have to write a book every day. But you can write a paragraph of a book every day.

You don't have to write a blog every day. But you can write a tweet every day.

By doing 1, number 2 becomes easy to implement. Plan for when you're sick. Why?

Because when you expect yourself to be sick at some point, that's when you become more creative.

You'll have content in your arsenal that you can still publish because you prepared for this moment. Not breaking your publishing streak does wonders for your confidence.

2 is more about thinking in systems rather than being a day-by-day thinker.

A true storyteller collapses time and sees the entire picture at once. To see the entire picture at once, it's all about being a superstar in the mind.

We are playing sports.
Just the mental kind.

Systematize your creativity, otherwise, you'll go mad.

Changing your Perception of Yourself

I recall how storytelling can change your perception of yourself as I was working on my Word Play book. This is a book that has 101 short stories, essays and insights that improves communication skills (currently available on Amazon).

One of the stories was about the beloved hype man.

In the story, I am supposed to go to a friend's birthday party in Orlando. I live in Tampa. Normally, the drive is 1.5 hours.

However, on this day, there was a car accident that was jamming up the road. What was supposed to be a 1.5-hour ride turned into a 3-hour ride from hell.

By the time I got to the party location, there wasn't any parking. My phone was about to die.

So, I had to park a far distance away and walk to the party location.

At this point, I'm tired, angry & just wanted to go to bed. But I had a long night of partying ahead of me.

When I got into the party, I saw how everyone was having fun. Others asked me what took so long. I told them about my story and my ride from hell.

They blankly stared at me, pretended they were listening and said, 'well, that's great, now it's time to party!'

They didn't listen.

Later in the event, I ran into the birthday boy. It was his night, but when he saw me, he was concerned with why it took me so long to arrive.

As I gave him bits of information to not bring his mood down, immediately, he was able to put the context together.

1.   He saw that I had been stuck in traffic.

2.	Had to park far away.
3.	And had been working all day.

The birthday boy gave me coffee and asked about my day.

Even though he was the star of the night, he treated me like the celebrity.

The birthday boy was the beloved hype man.

Not a guy who was jumping up and down, acting like a clown. Instead, the kind of guy who noticed the little details which are often overlooked.

'So, what does this have to do with storytelling?'

As I shared this story, I got the **full picture** of how being stuck in traffic was going to teach me a social skills lesson about the beloved hype man.

In the future, when I got stuck in traffic, I didn't get agitated as quickly.

Instead, my mind defaulted into thinking if this was the beginning of another lesson?

Sometimes, a lesson is presented.
Other times, the lesson is not presented

immediately.

Since telling that story, *I became calmer.*

I don't know about you, but for me, that's an amazing concept. Content creation is spilling over to the world of emotional intelligence.

It's sort of like you are dreaming, and the dream turns into a nightmare. The boogie monster is chasing you. You and your friend are running for your lives.

As the boogie monster is picking up speed, your friend suddenly stops running.

You look at your friend and ask:
'What are you doing?? Are you crazy?? The monster is going to catch us!!'

That's when your friend is like:
'Haha, this is just a dream bro. The monster can't do anything to us.'

You look at him, confused.

That's when your friend starts running towards the boogie monster.
Guess what?

The boogie monster starts running away.

Now, you are looking at this entire environment around you and are like:
'Whoa, is this really a dream?'

Yeah, it is. You're still perceiving the same data, however, the **narrative** has changed.

That's what storytelling does to the mind. It allows you to change your perception of yourself and your surroundings.

There was a famous film director who said:
'Humans are meant to express the truth. That's all film is. The expression of truth in different forms. The only difference between me and you is that I can articulate the truth and you can't.'

Thus far, we haven't talked too much about settings, conflicts, and plot building and all that.

We will soon.

But for the time being, our goal is to get engulfed in the fundamentals and fall in love with that.

When someone jumps straight into long division without falling in love with basic division, they can't help but give themselves a headache.

Storytelling is a just a string of ideas.

The more ideas you string together, the more you begin changing your perception.

Neurolinguistic programming

Changing perception is what all of self-improvement is built on. They just go about it in different ways.

Have you wondered why someone is spending their money trying to change their weight?

Why they are going to boot camps to become a pickup artist?

Why they are paying a coach to teach them business?

All these decisions stem from the desire to change their perception of themselves.

'What do you think is one of the best ways to change perception of ourselves?'

Through words.
What are words?

'Uh...I don't know, words?'

Don't you hate that...
When you Google a definition and they give you the definition of the word that you were looking to understand.

What does castrate mean?
When you castrate something.

Duh!

Seriously though, words are what I call *perception programmers*.

With the right use of a word, our perception can entirely change. The words we use create imagery which eventually influence our nerve impulses.

Elephant.

What do you picture?
'An elephant.'

Purple elephant.
What do you see?
'A purple elephant.'

Is a purple elephant real?
'No.'

Then how are you seeing it?
'I have no clue.'

Words allow you to defy the laws of physics. A great storyteller makes a mockery out of the laws of physics, repeatedly.
o   With words, we can change our perception.

But there is a catch.
'Which is?'
The words **need** to be personal to us.

If I just say, 'googlyeyedmooglytoogly.'

Your mind cannot process it. That's because the phrase does not resonate with your identity.

When understanding the mind, understand the different features of it.

The features of the mind include:
o   Intellect
o   Memory
o   Identity
o   Sensory processing system

Even though I am labeling them as separate; they

all function together just like the fingers in your palm all work as a unified system.

We are momentarily separating them to build further understanding of each component.

Memory

Memory is the storehouse of experiences. Everything that we have been through is in the memory somewhere. Without the memory, each day would feel like a new day, literally.

Memory makes a great servant, but an awful master.

Plenty of people allow memory to be their master. That's why they repeat the same mistakes of the past in new moments of the future.

Intellect

Intellect is the true or false sector of the mind. That's all critical thinking is:
  o   True or false done in iterations.

1. Cat is an animal - true
2. Dog is an animal - true
3. Cats and dogs are animals - true
4. Dogs and cats are the same - false

At the fundamental level, it's just true and false happening in intervals.

Identity

Identity is also known as the ego. This is where our emotions and narratives are stored.

This is when we get our memory and identify with certain parts of it. Our name, we identify with. Our job title, we identify with. Our family, we identify with.

Anything that causes some sort of feeling is seen as relevant information & our ego identifies with it.

If a storyteller wants to have someone's ears, see what they predominantly identify with. That's what it means to 'know your audience.'

Also, the identity is something that is personal to each human being.

Even though groupthink is becoming more popular in our era, make sure you take the effort to talk to each human as an individual. A storyteller does this because they understand how the mind works.

Sensory Processing System

Before you runaway in horror, this phrase is not that difficult. When we perceive life, we are perceiving data, not the actual items.

A famous philosopher once said that humans are just perceiving their nervous systems.

It'd be a disaster if a lamp actually entered your eye.

Instead, light bounces of the lamp and you perceive the light, aka: data streams. The *data streams* are inputted through your eyes, organized in the boundaries of space, time & causation, then you perceive it.

When I say that the data is organized into space, time, and causation, what I mean is that you are capable of seeing different forms and objects rather than just a blob of light.

One example is your cellphone. All you're really seeing is a blob of light. But the light is organized in different shades to create the illusion of buttons that you can click. Each button seems separate from one another which creates a spacing. That's similar to how human perception works.

What's unique is that even with the eyes closed, the sensory processing system still functions, aka: dreaming.

During dreams, we aren't getting light from the external world.

Instead, our mind pulls memories from our memory banks and creates an alternate reality with the same rules of perception.

The main difference from a dream and reality is the degree of involvement of our nervous system. For one, our eyes are open. For the other, our eyes are closed.

So, the 4 components of the mind are:
- o   Intellect
- o   Memory
- o   Identity
- o   Sensory processing system

All of them are meant to work in unison.
However, for many people, their components are **not** working in unison.

Instead, the parts of their mind conflict with each other.

'No way!'
Yep.

For example, any fear.

Intellectually, you know the fear isn't that bad. Public speaking to be more specific.

The talk is only 5 minutes. However, the identity is colliding with basic intellect and says, 'no, public speaking in front of familiar faces can kill you. Avoid it.'

A storyteller tames the identity.
 o   Identity = Ego.
This is our perception of ourselves.

This is why in an earlier section, we talked about being secondary to our idea. Our goal as storytellers is to objectify ourselves. The more we objectify ourselves, the more we expand beyond our identity and perceive life for what it is.

We need to become secondary to an idea. Allow the idea to be empowering rather than draining.

The mind is not meant to be the master, it's meant to be a servant to **only one grand idea.**

Some people call that grand idea:
 o   God
 o   Their business
 o   North star

o   Mission

This is the theme that guides thoughts.

When we get in the habit of articulating the idea from multiple angles, that's when it becomes easier to tame the identity.

When you tame the identity, that's when neurolinguistic programming begins.

Stories in Conversations

I'm sure you know a few people who tell fantastic tales in conversations. They are telling a story and others shut up and listen.

You may feel like the exact opposite.

When you tell a story, it feels like others are in a rush to interrupt you and talk over you.

Why?

That's not only a problem you face. Even charismatic storytellers often get spotlight jacked too.

'Spotlight jacked?'
Yes. When they have their spotlight taken away and it is never returned.

When interacting with humans, do not be

surprised by chaos, expect it. Expect that there is going to be some jerk who takes away your spotlight.

That's not even fully fair. Some of these people are not really jerks, they are just unaware.

Remember, humans are walking talking information systems. As you were telling a story about your cat, they resonated with that point. It's because from their database (experiences) they too have a cat.

At first, they want to contribute to your point to build further rapport. But overtime, they got so entrenched in the story that they forgot they took the spotlight away in the first place.

All good!
Continue on.

How do you tell a story in a conversation?

You go in with the intent of leading with context first. The content will fall out of the context.

Stories are used to build rapport and build connection with others. Therefore, to understand what type of story to tell, it's smart to understand the environment you're in.

If you enter an Uber ride and tell a story of your childhood, the driver will look at you in confusion.

But if the Uber driver asks:
'Yo man, how was your day?'

Now you have been given the context to tell a story about your day.

A story is a string of ideas.

When you are talking to another human, there is an alternate mode you want to get into.
'The mode of what?'
Edutainment.

o   Edutainment blends education and entertainment.

Education is to make someone aware, and entertainment is to fill the story with your personality.

I knew this one girl who was very sarcastic. She would always make sarcastic comments and see if you could keep up with her wit.

That was something that I had no desire of doing. I just wanted to have a conversation and leave it at that. I'm not trying to have a mental jousting competition with you.

However, that was **her** personality, and she didn't sway from it.

Was that the most socially intelligent thing to do? *Depends on who you ask.*

From her perspective, I respect that. If that's your authentic personality, then stand by it when you're telling your stories.

When telling stories in a conversation, it's all about making the story an arm rather than a horn.

o   If I tell you to envision yourself with horns, that will require cognitive effort.
o   If I tell you to envision yourself with arms, that will not require cognitive effort.

You'll be like:
'Well, I already have arms, so I will envision what I normally see in the mirror.'
Correct.

Same with telling stories.
We are not trying to make it seem like we have horns, because our goal is to reduce the cognitive effort that's needed.

Before telling stories in conversations, we should be living and breathing stories at this point.

- o   Collecting & clarifying nodes.
- o   Creating connections.
- o   Building insights.
- o   Practicing the art of speaking & writing.

That's when telling stories in a conversation is more natural.

The less cognitive effort an activity takes, the easier it becomes to incorporate your personality into it.

That's why practice is king.

I've worked with a few people in getting their YouTube channels started. They are typically introverted entrepreneurs who want to get in front of the camera to share their message.

These introverted entrepreneurs are a hub of knowledge. But they need to move out of their own way when it comes down to delivering their content.

That's why they practice telling the stories, more and more. At first, they say they feel uncomfortable.

I ask them what they are speaking to.
They say, 'a camera.'

I ask them how it was like when they met their best friend for the first time. Were they immediately hitting it off?
'No, we needed some time to get warmed up to each other,' they said.

Okay, so if you need to get warmed up to humans, then what makes you think that you won't need to get warmed up to a lifeless machine??

They eventually understood the importance of putting in the reps so storytelling can feel like an arm rather than a horn.

That's what it's like to tell stories in conversations.

It's a game of practicing.

Some people will get it.
Some people won't.

Rejection is the predecessor for more creativity.

Handling Rejection

When I hear stories about big named comedians, I try to see if I can find an interview of their come up.

That's when they often have these interviews where they talk about how they had to work their way up.

For years, they were getting booed, and they couldn't stand it.
But for every *boo*, there was also some applause.

Eventually, they learned that comedy was a game where you wanted to embrace rejection.

Hot and cold beats warm any day of the week.
Storytelling is a lot like that.

Imagine you're a salesman whose time is money.

Then you probably want to know from the get-go if someone is interested or not. If they are not interested, fine, just let me know asap so you quit wasting my time.

What's annoying is when someone acts interested but isn't. This person is warm.

A warm person creates false hope in your mind. You're putting more and more effort to working for this person's sale for them to eventually be like:
'Eh, I'm not interested.'

Why didn't you tell me this from the get-go?!

With storytelling, we want to:
  o   Play to win.
  o   Rather than play not to lose.

Too many people in conversations tell stories trying not to lose. They think:
'Hmm, let me pussyfoot in a way so incase my story falls flat, I don't create an awkward silence.'

That's when their decision tree reduces.

For a quick refresher, a decision tree is the number of options available to the mind at a moment.

An expanded decision tree is an expanded number of nodes that we can hop from to build creativity.

It's like a monkey swinging from branch to branch with the wind flying across its face. The monkey feels ALIVE because it realizes that the jungle is his.

Now contrast that with a monkey who only has a few trees available, and the branches are weak.

The monkey wonders if swinging on the branches would be smart if the branches are not sturdy?

So, as it's trying to swing from branch to branch, it keeps second guessing and thinking:
'Geez, I hope I don't break the branch and fall to my demise.'

This is how a lot of storytellers are telling stories and it's a damn shame.
   o   If someone doesn't like your story, oh well.
   o   If someone likes your story, great.

Have that mindset.

That mindset is only built from practice. An abundance mindset is built through reps.

Let's go back to the sales example.

That mindset is only built from practice. An abundance mindset is built through reps.

Let's go back to the sales example.

Imagine if this salesman only has 4 people in his pipeline. All 4 people have given a flat out 'no' to the salesman.

At this point, the salesman's confidence is hurt, and his narrative mind has been impacted.

The narrative mind creates thoughts like:
o   'Geez, am I good enough? '
o   'How come **everyone** is telling me no?'
o   'Maybe mom and dad were right, I don't have what it takes to be a salesman.'

Now contrast this with the salesman who has 50 leads in his arsenal.

16 say no.
12 don't respond.
12 say yes.
10 say maybe.

Is this salesman questioning his self-worth? He has 4 times as many no's than before.

But he is still composed because his decision tree

is expanded. There's a sense of FEARLESS-NESS that is built from reps.

That's why I hate the quantity vs. quality debate.
   o   Quantity leads to quality.
Especially in creative fields.

Which is why you should practice storytelling anywhere. If you're waiting for the perfect time to tell a story in a conversation, then you'll be waiting for a long time.

After being assimilated in the conversation, you'll have a general understanding of the context of the conversation.

A lot of times, there is little to no intellectual effort needed to tell a story. It's a primal desire that just happens. We want to avoid being long winded and yapping away.

We want to get to the point.
Each time we tell a story, we allow ourselves to:
   o   Build rapport with the other party.
   o   Plus, we show social dominance.

Picture those TVs shows where there is a person of power talking to a person who works for the person of power.

Who is telling the story and who is listening?

It's the CEO that's telling the story to the janitor. This is a powerful move because the janitor may want to be in the same spot as the CEO one day.

And for the janitor to rise, he must absorb the knowledge of the CEO.

For the CEO to have risen to his level, he must've learned that lectures rarely work.

So, the CEO blends real world lessons into fun tales and comedy. He is teaching the janitor without the janitor knowing that he is being taught.

The reason that the CEO is effortlessly telling stories is because he has talked to people of all shapes and sizes on his journey to the top.

Nowadays, he feels composed.

The only way to overcome the feeling of rejection is through more reps, not less.

Play to win and quit playing not to lose.

Storytelling Challenge: 1 Minute Story

I want to introduce a fun game that you can play whenever you're bored.

o   Tell a story in 1 minute or less.

Your story only needs a character, conflict, and lesson.

Example:

'Johnathan was having a good morning. Little did he know, that was about to change. Jonathan came to work and noticed all his items were packed with a pink slip on his desk. A pink slip, really?? He gave the company 32 years of his life, and this is how they repay him?

He furiously picks up the pink slip to read it.

When he reads the slip, he realizes that he isn't getting fired. Instead, it was a birthday card with a note saying:
'Happy birthday John! We decided it was time for you to get the big office!'

  o   Character = Jonathan.
  o   Conflict = A potential firing.
  o   Lesson = Don't rush to conclusions so soon.

This is a creative exercise. Avoid overthinking the formulas and frameworks.

All you need is 1 minute (or less) and a character, conflict, and lesson.

'Hey Armani, why only 1 minute? Why not give me 10 minutes?'
Because this allows you to flex your creativity even more.

In the land of creativity, brevity is a sign of intelligence.
It's much harder to share a compelling 1-minute story versus a 10-minute story.

A 1-minute story guarantees you will seamlessly

be able to learn 10-minute stories, but the opposite is not always true.

'Gotcha. Why the character, conflict & lesson variables to be exact?'
That's a great question.

The reason we are choosing these variables is because it is the **bare minimum** needed to articulate human experiences.

The focal point of storytelling = Human Experiences.

Since we are focused on human experiences, we have a character for that reason. A character can be fictional or nonfictional, that part does not matter.
The character is only a conduit to express a truth.

As you're getting started, I recommend making yourself the main character of these 1-minute stories.

This allows you to practice storytelling AND introspection skills.

The next thing is the conflict.
The conflict of a story is like the cream to an Oreo.

Imagine if someone gave you an Oreo with just the 2 brown crackers. They told you they kept the creme for themselves.

You'd feel betrayed!
What kind of savage is this??

It's the creme that holds the Oreo together. Likewise, it's the conflict that holds the story together.

Why?

First, let's use a tad bit of common sense. Imagine that you were hearing a story that went something like this:

'John's day was going well. In the morning, he woke up filled with energy. In the middle of the day, just when he thought the day couldn't get any better, it did! He was given a promotion and was more enthusiastic than ever. By the time he came home, he was ready to celebrate his already great day. That's when he heard even more great news! Apparently, he won the most recent lottery. A fantastic day indeed.'

The end.

Doesn't that feel strange?
Doesn't it feel like someone gave you 2 brown

crackers with the creme missing?

'Whoa, it kind of does.'
That's why the conflict is needed.
The conflict engages curiosity.

'Do you think curiosity is primal?'
Absolutely.

The mind is built for curiosity. This is known as the *law of closure*.

If you want to see the law of closure in action, then hold your index fingers 1 inch apart from each other in front of your face.

There will be this primal **desire** to make the fingers tips touch. Once you make them touch, there will be a **strong** sensation in the chest which indicates: mission accomplished.

In storytelling, conflict & curiosity go hand in hand.

The second your conflict is introduced is the second the consumer's curiosity is engaged.

Now for the last part, the lesson.
   o   Not all stories need a good ending.
   o   Not all stories need a bad ending.
   o   But all stories need a lesson.

A lesson is an insight.
This is us closing the loop.

A lesson speaks to someone's heart and is beyond the intellect alone.

Within your practice of creating lessons through stories, you learn to teach your mind how to think in themes. The theme allows you to become a big picture storyteller.

That's all you need by the way.
1-minute stories.

These 1-minute stories will add up over time. The more they add up, the more you can process information regarding all other topics.

The more stories you tell, the more stories you are capable of telling.

Telling Stories in Meetings

You're officially a leader.
Maybe you have a job where you got a recent promotion, or you started a business.

Now what?

How is it that you command these people and capture their narrative mind?

This is a question that we want to give ourselves some time to think about. Let's brainstorm together.

How do you convince people who are working because they are 'have to', to follow your lead?

'Give them bonuses?'
What if you don't have additional funds to give them bonuses?

'Um, force them to do the work?'
What if that leads to a coup?

'I'll fire them if they dare backstab me!'
What if you're at the stage where these workers have specialized knowledge and replacing them will cause you to miss tons of deadlines?

'I don't know then. What's your strategy?'
We use the art of the narrative.

Your life as a storyteller will be much easier if you assumed that people had a big sticker on their forehead which said:
'What's in it for me?'

If you just saw this imaginary sticker, you'd stop with these ridiculous lectures.

When you see them with the imaginary sticker on their forehead, you'd talk to them on a personal level.

I had this job a few years ago in a prestigious company. However, the culture was not the best.

Upper management wanted to bond with the workers more. This is why the management began hosting more townhalls.

At first, attending these townhalls were optional.

Later, they became mandatory because no one would attend.

A townhall is when a bunch of the workers get in a shared location and hear upper management give updates about the status of the company.

We had these upper management members suited up:
  o   They were reading slide after slide.
  o   Showing the forecasting data & other 'riveting' metrics.
  o   And telling us why we should be happy.

Then they opened the floor for a question-and-answer section.

This was painful to say the least. We'd keep getting reprimanded with:
'Seriously guys? No one has a question? Come on, don't be shy!'

These grown upper management talking to other grown employees like little kids.

That's when the employees reluctantly got up one by one and forced themselves to ask a question.

The managers were happy to not be greeted by dead silence.

Needless to say, these townhalls were a waste of time. Upper management practiced their communication skills & the workers had to force themselves to stay awake for 1.5 hours.

Want to know what's scary?
If you're in the corporate world, this sounds too familiar. That's how plenty of meetings are hosted.

A few months later, we had a shift in management. One of the new managers was this guy named Ed.
He was from the Bronx and was a in your face New York guy.

One time, he had a floor meeting where he wanted us to meet him at a pond.

Outside of our building, there was this beautiful pond with a bunch of koi fish. This was an area where a lot of the workers would walk during their breaks. But it wasn't a place we'd ever host meetings.

We went to the meeting location. Rather than there being 100+ people like there were in the townhalls, there were only 20 people.

Ed came by with pizza and donuts.

Then he told us what his plan was for the upcoming year.

Midway in, he noticed all the workers were sitting up straight and being stiff. That's when he said:
'Relax fellas, this is a chill event. No need to have a stick up your ass, haha.'

He was this larger-than-life presence and had a contagious laugh.

The managers in the townhall wouldn't have spotted the stiff body language because they would have been too focused on their PowerPoints.

But Ed immediately noticed everyone's body language because he read the stickers on our foreheads which said:
'What in it for me?'

Notice what I said…
I didn't write:
'What's in it for us?'

Ed wasn't talking to team by team.
Because then his delivery would still be too formal. He wouldn't have been addressing someone's primal desires if he was talking to 'teams.'

He was talking to individuals.

o   Great storytellers speak to one person at a time.

o   Average storytellers speak to a crowd.

One of the lines that Ed told me that stuck out was:
'I'm going to make it easier than ever for ambitious people to rise up in the company.'

That was a very polarizing statement.

Because let's face it, when a company scales, most people don't have ambition. They are taking it day by day so they can retire.

But there are a few people who do want to rise. However, there are so many office politics that they begin wondering:
'Why even bother?'

With that one statement from Ed, he did 2 things:
  1.   He lit a fire in the asses of those who were ambitious.
  2.   He made the zombies who were taking it day by day question their decisions.

That's what happens when you talk to 1 person at a time.

You inspire pockets of people & those pockets of people turn into a herd in a matter of time.

Why Storytelling is a Must for a Leader

Get rid of the 'once upon a time' notion. Normally, when someone is thinking storytelling, they are thinking too much in terms of fantasy.

Read this book a few times. There hasn't been any thing that has escaped the domain of practicality.

Everything being discussed will aid you if you deal with humans because humans are information processing systems.

Stories are built into the psyche.

We don't want to be general with our language, we want to be precise.

It's one thing to learn the art of a field. It's

another thing to learn the science of a field.

But only a rare few can combine the 2 until art & science become one.

A storyteller and a leader go hand in hand. What separates a boss from a leader?
o   A boss is a title.
o   A leader is a character trait.

A boss forces people to work.
While a leader inspires others into action.

To inspire someone, we don't need to jump on a table and give them a rah-rah speech. As a matter of fact, we can be tamed.

We need to give them clarity.

I want to give you a scenario, and I want you to think about what the lesson is. Cool?
'Yeah, cool. Let me hear it!'

Imagine there is a boring YouTuber who is speaking in a monotoned voice to the camera. He has 0 enthusiasm, his shirt is dirty & he seems like he's about to fall asleep any second.

This YouTuber is giving a talk about how to carry yourself in a networking event if you're shy.

o   100 people watch this YouTube video.
o   99 close the YouTube video in disgust.
o   1 person is glued to the video.

The reason that 1 person is glued to the video is because he is shy. Plus, he has a networking event coming up in 10 minutes.

Therefore, he ignores the YouTuber's lack of charm and is still **inspired** by the content.

Can you give me your rationale for why something like this occurred?
'Is it because the YouTuber reminded the shy guy of himself?'

That's close, but can you get a bit more specific?
'The YouTuber gave him clarity?'
Yes!!!!

When you give someone clarity, you give them confidence.

A leader must be able to give clarity at will.

If you can give someone clarity, they will overlook a lot of your flaws and look to you with inspiration.

Here's the thing a lot of leaders do when their workers are not inspired:

o They huddle them up in a cramped-up room and start pounding away more deadlines and ultimatums to the workers.

This only irritates the workers and drains their enthusiasm.

How much more effective would it be if the leaders would take some time to teach the workers how their roles serve the entire system?

Right now, the workers are working, but have no clue of the purpose behind their work. This happened to me before.

There was this one internship where I was making a bunch of Excel sheets. My manager was very nice, but busy as hell. He would just keep giving me random Excel sheets to make. So, I kept making them.

After a certain point, I was bored because I had no clue **why** I was doing what I was doing.

One day, there was a woman named Jennifer Mullet who came to my cube. She looked just like Ellen DeGeneres.

'Are you Arman Chowdhury?'
'I am,' I responded.
'Come with me,' she said.

She took me to her office and said:

'Thank you so much for your Excel sheets. Ron has been sending them to me. Do you know how much you've helped my staff?'

I had no clue what the hell she was talking about.

That's when she started to create a bunch of boxes on the whiteboard. She drew at least 10 rectangular boxes.

In one of the boxes, she put my team's name in it. Slowly, she began filling in the boxes with the other team names.

Then she started linking the boxes together. Once she began linking them together, she was telling me why she was sequencing them in that particular order.

'So, EMEA impacts APAC & APAC impact USA, blah blah blah…'

Slowly but surely, I was seeing **exactly** what she was doing.

'You know your Excel sheets? I gave them to all these different teams. For the past few months, we were having a lot of miscommunications because we all go by different time zones.

But your Excel sheets allowed us to follow a standardized format. This has saved us a lot of time.'

Just imagine!!! I was working on these Excel sheets like a mindless puppet for so long without have the slightest clue as to what I was doing.

When Jennifer gave me the BIG picture understanding of what I was doing, I felt a flurry of sensations in my heart and my skin felt warm.

At the end of my internship, I had a meeting with upper management to share what value I added to the company. This meeting would decide if I got a fulltime offer in the future or not.

I was able to share the value I provided based on the conversation I had with Jennifer. She gave me clarity.

The thing is that a lot of workers have 0 clue what purpose they serve to the bigger picture.

This is when you:
  o   Compartmentalize
  o   Dominate

Compartmentalize allows you to talk to the worker/or teams 1 on 1. You don't always have to have a big get together when you are leading with stories.

153

Instead, getting the *right* people for the right event is all it takes to make an impact.

Jennifer didn't bring 240 other people to her 1 on 1 meeting with me. Instead, it was just me and her, which allowed the meeting to be impactful.

As for dominate, it's back to the sticker on the forehead trick:
'What's in it for me?'

Jennifer wasn't over here babbling away about the work she does with her team. She simply shared the big picture to give me more clarity.

That's what stories do to someone.
It gives them clarity.
It takes them out of the forest & gives them a bird's eye view.

That's how a leader inspires.

Are PowerPoints Evil?

PowerPoints often become the punching bag for those who know how to speak.
'Me? Nah, I don't need a PowerPoint. Those are for wimps! I'm already a great speaker.'

I have a different philosophy. I think the Power-Point is not the enemy, it's just a tool. Therefore, it should be perceived as a tool.

The only thing that makes the PowerPoint bad is when the tool is treated like a master. It often becomes the master when the user does not understand the fundamentals of storytelling.

Storytelling is meant to provide clarity into a messy field.

Others have a 'what's in it for me?' mentality. Rather than hammering them with irrelevant information that does not address their narrative mind, address their narrative mind.

The way we do that is by allowing our Power-Point to be something that provides more **under-standing & depth** to what we are saying.

Words are a great tool. But using too many words is a fast way to make sure that your message falls flat.

o   Avoid using 40 words when 18 will do the trick.

PowerPoints for a storyteller is very similar to index cards for a public speaker.

Are index cards bad? No.
But if all you do is read of the index cards, then that's bad!!!

If your index cards were set on fire, would you still be able to give the speech?

No?
Then rethink your approach.

If you answered:
'Yeah, I could still give a speech even if my index cards were set on fire.'
Then keep doing what you are doing.

Likewise, have the same philosophy with a Power-Point.

Can you give your storytelling presentation even if the PowerPoint slides did not to work?

Not to be the bearer of bad news, but there will be plenty of times when there will be technical issues that render your PowerPoint useless.

If your PowerPoint is useless, are you useless as well?

If so, then you need to rethink your approach.

When we approach the building of the Power-Point with the intention of:
'Okay, this is only a *tool* that will help me teach the audience.'
That's when we give ourselves the permission to be more creative in our approach.

Through clarity, our personality can shine through the brightest.

From the right attitude, top tier insights become autopilot.

What Do You Do?
Challenge

Let's do a storytelling challenge to give our creative muscles a workout.

Don't you hate the question:
'What do you do?'

Some people will say, yes.
Some people will say, no.

The people who hate this question are often very creative. They do not only do one thing. Instead, they wear multiple hats.

I knew this one website developer who hated that question. At first, I didn't get why he hated it so much. Just say you're a *web developer* and keep it moving.

The more I got to know this fellow, the more I

saw how he was more than just a website developer. He was a web developer, businessman, content creator and much more.
Therefore, the question was difficult to answer.

There is another group of people who find it easy
to answer the 'what do you do?' question.

They will seamlessly say a realtor, engineer,
doctor without second thought. They say their
profession on autopilot like they announce their
name.

Here is the challenge:

If you consider yourself as the creative type, then
I want you to give a 1–4-minute story talking
about what you do.

Keep your ego out of it. I don't need to know
every little crevice of what you do.

Assume I have a low attention span & I'm just
quickly asking you this question as a sake of
formality.

However, fill up your story with a true representation of what you do:
  o   Focus on simplicity.
  o   Provide some analogies.
  o   Keep the talk interactive.

For the other group of people who answer the 'what would you do' question with ease, I want you to reframe.

I want you to answer, 'what purpose does your work serve?'

Sure, you are a realtor.
But what purpose does that role serve to the bigger picture?

Sure, you are an engineer.
But what purpose does that role serve to the bigger picture?

And sure, you are a doctor.
But what purpose does that role serve to the bigger picture?

By doing this, you develop a deeper understanding of your field and get a holistic perspective of your work.

Recap:
For creative fields, explain what you do in a simple, concise way that engages the listener and paints an accurate depiction of the hats you wear.

For non-creative fields, explain the purpose your field serves to the bigger picture.
4-5 minutes.

Creative Challenge 2

What, you thought we were done?

Now is the time for another creative storytelling challenge:

Here is the following prompt:

'There is a purple hippo who what wants to become a dog. The hippo's desire is to be a pet to a human like a dog. How does the hippo go about its journey towards the transformation? Is the hippo successful?'

Take this story wherever you want to take it. I will give you some optional recommendations.

1. Try to do it on a Microsoft document rather

than handwriting it. This will allow you to flow.

2. Create like no one will read it & edit like everyone will read it.

a. If you have trouble creating, reduce the timer.

i. Pressure + Time = Anxiety

ii. Pressure - Time = Creativity

Once you are complete, read your writing out loud.

Power of Analogies

There was one-time I was working in an Aerospace company.

Your boy was only making a measly 8 dollars an hour. However, it was the experience that was key.

I worked as a systems engineer, learned what the software engineers did, worked with the hardware engineers and much more. It was a blast.

The other students in the College of Engineering were working great internships too.

But the idea that I was getting experience in an aerospace company made them feel some type of way. The aerospace industry was viewed in a prestigious light in the College of Engineering.

bunch of the students asked me what I did.

That's when I began communicating in a way that was considered confusing.

'Well, I was creating pressure systems for the airplane pilots so they got knowledge of their surroundings to navigate the altitude and longitude of the plane.'

Blah blah blah.

These enthusiastic students now looked back at me with a bored face.
'Nice.'

Then they went back to work.

Wait a minute. This was not the reaction I was expecting. I thought I was going to get more praise.

My close friend, Tommy, let me have it.
'I have no clue what you're saying, Armani. Dumb it down for me.'

Those 5 words changed my life when it came to storytelling.

DUMB IT DOWN FOR ME.

When he told me that, it's as though a bunch of

new thought waves were unleashed.

'Hey Tommy, you drive, right?'
'Yeah, I drive.'

'Okay, imagine driving with no side mirrors or rearview mirrors. How would that feel?'
'Bro, I'd be scared man. It'd feel like I lost my perspective.'

'Right. Now imagine you didn't have a speedometer either. How would you feel?'
'Dude, I'd drive **super** cautious then.'

'Would you feel confident driving the car?'
'Hell no! I'd be driving like a wimp.'

That's when I eagerly responded with:
'Exactly. Well, my company provided pilots with more perspective. We gave them tools that allowed them to know about their surroundings in more detail.'

'Whoa, that makes so much more sense!!' said Tommy.

Boom.
   o   DUMB IT DOWN FOR ME.

Stupid people try to act smarter than they are.

Smart people act dumber than they are.

Stupid people are unaware of their behavior.
Smart people are perfectly aware.

Do you want to learn how to tell better stories?
Here's a mental hack:
   o   Whatever topic you are talking about, add
'for dummies' at the end.

Public speaking, for dummies.
Storytelling, for dummies.
Podcasting, for dummies.

When you add 'for dummies' at the end, this
engages the simplification muscle, and you begin
to measure success based on how well your message is being digested by others.

Analogies speak directly to the subconscious
mind.

Let's review the 4 components of the mind. There
is the:
   o   Intellect
   o   Memory
   o   Identity
   o   Sensory processing system

If I'm using language that does not remotely

to their memory, do you think they will be able to perceive it?

Hell no.

So, we want to communicate in a simple way that engages their memory.

When we engage their memory, we automatically engage all other parts of them.

Any bubba can drive or at least understands the basic components of how driving happens. That's why Tommy was able to pick up my analogy.

One time, there was a spiritual teacher who was talking about how we are all servants of God. I wanted to hear this guy because he seemed like a good storyteller.

He started telling a story about what happens when a component does not want to serve the entire system.

He said that's like the hand who develops a lot of pride and is like:
'I don't need the body anymore.'

So, the hand asks the body to cut it off.

When the body cuts it off, the hand suddenly

becomes lifeless, and the entire body suffers as well.

This spiritual teacher was stressing the importance of serving the entire system. When you serve the system, you get served too.

When the hand uses the spoon to feed the body, that's when the body gives the hand nutrition too. Much better than being lifeless.

Whether I agreed with this man's philosophy or not was not the point.

What happened as he was telling the story through analogy format was that I was **hooked.**

I could completely interpret what he was saying. Nothing he was saying was defying logic.

This moment showed me that analogies are the language of the subconscious mind.

When you ask the average bubba what analogies are, they start reciting the definition of 'similes' and 'metaphors.'

After they recite the definition, they look back at you with pride on their face. All they are doing is parroting a definition your way.

But they aren't giving true understanding.

To give true understanding, understand that at a core level, we process life though:
   o   Images and feelings.

Imagery are the thought waves and feelings are what thought waves we bring awareness to.

Analogies cut through all the noise and speak to the primal sides of a human. Therefore, practice analogies.

Quick disclaimer.

To share analogies on something, you must be knowledgeable in the field.

If you want me to give you analogies on marine life biology, I won't be able to because I don't know much about marine life biology.

When you are practicing the 'for dummies' trick to gather analogies, make sure you are knowledge-able on the field.

Great Storytellers are Fishers

Do you find it difficult to express yourself?

I know I used to find it very difficult.
I felt like it was impossible.

To make matters worse, it's like the universe had a way of putting me in situations where I had to speak up.

To make that situation even worse, there was always some smartass who would ask the question:
'Why are you so quiet?'

This question would make me livid & sad.

If they asked:
'Why are you an alien?'

Then I would have laughed.

But when they called me quiet, it hurt my feelings because I knew it was the truth.

For the next couple of years, I wanted to master communication skills.

For the past couple of years, I have:
- o   Given over 50 speeches.
- o   Emceed 6 events.
- o   Recorded over 400 YouTube videos.
- o   Wrote over 340 blogs.
- o   Recorded over 350 podcasts.
- o   Wrote over 60,000 tweets.
- o   Wrote 10 plus books.

And much more.

'What did you learn from all of this?'
That great storytellers are great fishers.

'What??'
Yes.

Picture a boy named Cobra.
Cobra is fishing.

In front of Cobra is this crystal-clear lake that you can see right through.

This lake is flowing in *one* direction.

Within this lake, a bunch of gray fish are swimming along the flow of the current.

Cobra's interest is not in the gray fish.
His interest is in the PINK fish.

Every now and then, there is a pink fish that swims along the lake. Cobra doesn't have a fishing pole, but he has his arm.

His goal is to capture as many pink fishes as he can.

Every now and then, when he spots the pink fish, he dives his hand in the lake and catches nothing.

Other times, he aims for the pink fish but captures a gray fish instead.

Cobra continues the same motion repeatedly.
1. Spot the pink fish.
2. Grab it.

Overtime, Cobra builds his proficiency. His reaction rate is getting faster, and he is capturing more pink fish & less gray fish.

This is exactly what it's like with storytelling.

Give your mind a topic to speak about.
When you give yourself a topic, you allow the

lake to flow in one direction. The lake is a representation of your mind.

If you just try speaking randomly, then all the fish's aka: thoughts, are not flowing in one direction.

With a story theme, that's when you create direction for the lake.

The gray fish represent thoughts.

But the pink fish are thoughts that have an emotional charge. Your goal is to articulate those pink fishes (thoughts with a charge).

You articulating your charged thoughts is equivalent to Cobra reaching his hand in the water, *over and over again.*

Sometimes, you'll try to capture the pink fish and end up catching nothing. Other times, you'll try to capture the pink fish and end up catching a gray fish. And other times, you'll catch the pink fish.

But in the process of articulating, over and over again, is how the storytelling muscle is built.

'Armani?'
Yes?

'How do I exactly spot the pink fish? Are you saying that I feel physical charges in my body?' That's correct.

The more personal the thought is to you, the more you feel a charge.

To prove this, say someone says a name that you don't know.

For *me, it's Jacobson.*

Now say someone says a named that I do know.

Arman.

I feel completely different sensations from **Jacobson** vs **Arman**. Both are letters stringed together. The main difference comes down to the physical sensations created by the letters.

Similarly, when we are speaking, there are certain thoughts which will stick out.

As you are getting warmed up with your fishing game, aim to start off with topics that are **personal** to you.

If you are talking about building a Stop sign, then you may not be able to spot any pink fish.

However, if you make Stop signs for a living, then this topic picks up a whole new life.

You may have a bunch of potential ways to handle this topic:
o   the dangerous conditions of how the Stop signs are made.
o   Why the Stop sign industry needs a union.
o   How you plan to start your own Stop sign businesses.

Bottom line?
Find topics that are personal to you.
Then find your pink fishes.

Stories and Brand Building

What is a brand?
Can you hold it?
Can you touch it?

Let's use Nike as an example.

How often do you hear Nike getting bootlegged?

The fake shoes look just like the real shoes. Unless you are a sneakerhead, then chances are you won't notice the difference.

Let's say someone gives you the fake shoes for your birthday. Initially, you are happy.

Later, a sneakerhead notifies you that the shoes are fake.

What next?

You're livid.

Knowing that this is not the **real** brand is what hurts the most. This brand that we resonate with is not physical, it's intangible.

The brand is the invisible feeling.

With storytelling, we must see how it relates to brand building.

Brand building is long term thinking. The longer term we think, the more we can develop a nuanced understanding of building a brand.

A story can exist without a brand.
But a brand cannot exist without a story.

In this era, there are media companies being formed by only 1 person.

This kid starts a YouTube channel, Tik Tok, Twitter page and starts to grow them.

You may be interested in that. Or let's say you don't want to be a personal brand but instead you want to create a story for your t-shirt company. How do you do that?

The way that we do that is by understanding one

of the most important words in storytelling. 'Which is?'

Resonation.
The reason resonation is so important is because it puts someone in the same frequency as you.
o   The brand message communicated effectively will make the recipient feel like you're talking directly to them.

The consumer is **convinced** that the brand was designed to fulfill the consumer's deepest desires.

To create a resonation point, we have to understand 2 predominant feelings:
o   Pleasure
o   Pain

Storytelling comes down to these 2 feelings. There are different types of these feelings.

For pain, there is:
o   Doubt
o   Betrayal
o   Anxiety
o   Sadness
Etc.

For pleasure, there is:

o   Gratitude
o   Winning
o   Happiness
o   Peace
Etc.

The goal of our brand story is to toggle from pain to pleasure and so on…

Let's do a simulation:

We are going to keep it super basic. Let's say the pain and pleasure dynamic that we want to create is *betrayal* and *happiness.*

'Gustavo was betrayed by his first love. To make it worse, his kids were ordered to be taken away from him. It took years for him to rebuild himself. Since then, he's a different man. He has worked out, met new people, improved his social skills and much more. Nowadays, Gustavo is happy & confident. He uses his brand to help other men deal with betrayal and rebuild their happiness.'

There are plenty of Gustavos out there. Gustavo may resonate with a handful of single fathers who just got demolished in the courtroom and lost custody of their children.

My ArmaniTalks brand message is pretty straightforward:

'I started off as a shy engineer. Communication skills helped me articulate my ideas and become more confident. '

Pain emotion was:
   o   Sadness in being shy.

Pleasure emotion is:
   o   Confidence in pursuing purpose with communication skills.

This pain/pleasure dynamic does not have to be basic by any means.

You can add tons of complexity to this formula. You can keep hopping from pain/pain/pleasure/pleasure/pain and so on.

Heck, you can use the pain/pleasure dynamic to write a book!!

View this as the skeleton. Once you have the general flow of the skeleton, the content takes care of itself.

A lot of prolific rappers rarely write down their music, they just listen to the beat. Then they feel the beat to get a general rhythm for how it sounds. Once they understand the general rhythm, that's when they put words on top of the beat.

For some reason, I used to think a rapper wrote the lyrics first and then put it on the beat later. I was surprised to see it was the opposite for a lot of rappers.

Similarly, with storytellers, we can get the general rhythm by creating our own pain/pleasure sequence.

Then we can superimpose the story on top.

Storytelling Exercise: Pain/Pleasure

I want you to create a story following the following rhythm

- o Pleasure - Enthusiasm
- o Pain – Fear
- o Pain - Anger
- o Pleasure - Fun

This exercise is advanced. If you find it too difficult, either challenge yourself to participate anyways or just stick with the first 2 bullets (enthusiasm & fear).

It can be a few sentences long or a few pages long.

Create without judgment & edit like a scaredy cat.

Brands Build Rapport

One time, I was in a Publix store, and I saw a deal for a bunch of pasta sauces that I never heard of.

When I looked at those sauces, I noticed they looked pretty good. However, until the moment of the sale, I had never looked towards those pasta sauces.

I would automatically go towards Ragu or Prego.

I do the same thing with Clorox wipes. That's my go-to option.

As I run the ArmaniTalks business, I see the multiple moving variables that are required to get a business up and running:
   o   The marketing.
   o   Product creation.
   o   Sales.

o   Communication.
o   Cash flow management.
And so much more.

Imagine if you are the creator of a product that competes with Ragu and Clorox. How annoying would it be to know that a bunch of potential customers are ignoring your existence on autopilot?

The only time you're acknowledged is when there is a massive sale.

It's easy to brush past this stuff. But when you look closely, it's something quite profound.

A brand needs to be consistent.
But how you're consistent is key.
o   You can be consistently above expectations.
o   You can be consistently below expectations.

I knew a haircut spot like that. I used to go to them when I was an undergrad student because I wanted to save some money and they would give student discounts.

Normally, the haircuts were 10 bucks. With the

student discounts, it came out to 7 bucks. The other haircut spots charged 25 dollars.

The low prices were great.
The haircuts were awful.

Every now and then, you'd get a quality cut.

But for the most part, the cuts were average at best. A lot of the times, you'd have to come home and finish the barber's job for them.

Later, I realized even 7 dollars was too much for this junk.

The barbers had developed into a brand, *just not the good kind.*

When communicating your brand story, you should envision yourself as your own customer.

I can't imagine how someone starts a business that they are not remotely interested in.

Actually, I can sort of get it. Some businesses are heavily centered around profit margins. Even though the business sucks, the money is great.

I see a lot of successful people say:
'I doubt the steel magnate is in love with steel.'

Hm…

I lowkey think he is in love with it if he's been consistent enough to rise to the top.

But assume that I'm wrong.
Assume that most people hate their business.

Well, suck it up and place yourself as the customer anyways.

With the ArmaniTalks brand, I'm a big fan of books. I used to hate reading back in the days though.

The reason I hated reading was because it felt like so much work. It felt like I had to go out of my way to read with a dictionary just to make sure I understood some big words.

These authors seemed so pompous. So much flowery language to say nothing.

This discouraged me.

I wanted to write books that I would have no problem consuming. Easy to understand and a breeze to go through.

People who often read my books say:
'Man, I started off with a few pages and out of

nowhere, I was on page 50.'

That's what I like to hear.
The ArmaniTalks brand for my hardcore readers is known as 'simple and to the point.'

This was a brand story that was an emergent property.

Take some time to look around a few items in your living facility. These brands are bought on autopilot and are rarely questioned. What are some brands like that you notice?

Dark Brands

Normally, when we think of *brands,* we may think of a warm and fuzzy feeling.
On the contrary, most brands are very polarizing.

Just like some people may like my writing because it's simple, others may hate it.
'Who is this guy? He sounds like a damn noob.'

To tell your brand story, you need to understand one key life law:
   o   To be loved by many, you will also be hated by many.

Where else is this more evident than in politics?

You'll see a person becoming a rabid fan while others become hateful.

One of the examples of a polarized brand is the name, Trump.

I recall there was this very quiet doctor who was normally soft spoken. He was an Indian guy who would normally keep the spotlight off him.

But the second he heard the name, *Trump*, his demeanor would change.

Suddenly, he became more vocal & hostile.

The person who bought up Trump would be talking in favor of the former president. That's when the quiet doctor got even more vocal and would aim to silence the Trump supporter.

Suddenly, the quiet doctor was getting in headed debates and making sure others thought twice before supporting Trump.

I looked back in amusement.

Here's a brand that is altering this guy's personality. He was completely unrecognizable.

A word represented a concept.
The concept activated his memory bank.
The memory bank came with the narrative of 'Anti Trump.'

The narrative caused him to go from soft spoken to vocal.

THE BRAND ALTERED HIS BEHAVIOR.

This may sound like a cool feature if you're a storyteller. You're thinking:
'I can brainwash these guys and get them to do whatever.'

If you can brainwash others, what do you think others are doing to you? Narratives are all around us. Something we often take as a fact, is a narrative when you peel back the layers.

You should look more at yourself. Are there certain phrases which *suddenly* piss you off?

If you want to mature, then question your generalities.

There are certain generalities where we just say, 'it has always been like that' and we may have a negative attitude towards it.

Well, if it's a generality and you don't know much about it, then the generalities serve as a brand for the mind.

Brands shortcut past your critical thinking to cause a behavior.

For example:

There may be plenty of sauces better than Ragu. Maybe other sauces are more affordable, use better ingredients & give you more quantity.

So?

In the world of brands, hardcore Ragu fans do not care about the logic.

4 faculties of the mind:
- o   Intellect
- o   Memory
- o   Identity
- o   Sensory processing system

Whenever the identity and intellect are in battle, the identity will often come out victorious.

If someone *identifies* with a certain brand, it doesn't matter if others *intellectually* try to convince them otherwise. The identity will shut down the logic.

I'm sure you've heard a lot of engineers tell you that a Droid is better than the iPhone in terms of processing power, battery life and other features.

iPhone users shut it down because they identify as an 'iPhone user.'
This is a smart time to question your generalities.

Storytelling Exercise: From General to Specific

What generality are you holding?
Think about it for some time.

Unless you are a perfect individual, you may have a couple of generalities that have formed.

I want you to create an explanation of the generality through the written or spoken format.

Take some time explaining the root cause of the generality, why you think it formed & what you will do about it now that you have noticed it.

A few examples of generalities are:
- o   All Republicans are ____
- o   All women are ____

o   Anyone who uses Tik Tok is ____
o   Droid users are ____

Keep searching.

Even if you don't find a generality that you hold, the process of looking for one will skyrocket your awareness.

Netflix and Fiction Books

o   Cancel Netflix accounts.

o   Your Netflix account isn't only 7 dollars, you pay with your time.

o   Congratulate Netflix for killing your dreams.

These are a lot of the quotes echoed in the self-improvement space.

Is it good advice?
Depends.

Advice that works for 1 group of people doesn't always work for another group of people.

NBA superstar, LeBron James, often watches 5 basketball games at the same time. He says that's equivalent to him reading a book.

Is that smart advice for the average Joe?
Probably not.

Martin Scorsese says that he spends hours watching film every day to build visual literacy.

Should a fat man who has been binging on Twinkies & Ho-Hos for the past couple of weeks spend hours every day watching film? Probably not.

Advice is subjective.

Netflix and fiction books are a CHEATCODE to improve storytelling skills.

I'm not saying that you consume content all day. What I am saying is to be reasonable in your consumption & I guarantee you'll learn how to tell better stories.

Think about it like this:
Netflix spends millions of dollars hiring screenwriters, movie directors, actors, and much more to create stories.

And you get the final output.

Why not use that as an opportunity to learn storytelling? You could argue that it's a masterclass on the subject.

By the way, you can take out Netflix for Amazon Prime, Hulu, HBO etc. I'm referring to any platform that hosts or creates content.

Most of these content platforms have tons of user data, so they are creating and hosting these films/sitcoms for a reason. Don't think the content just 'ended up' there.

You don't only have to watch new content, check out the classics too.

No lie, I've been rewatching Breaking Bad recently.

I've watched Breaking Bad for a total of 3 times throughout the years.

   o   The first time I watched it, I thought it was overrated.

   o   The second time I watched it, I thought it was underrated.

   o   The third time I watched it, I thought it was flawless.

For my most recent time watching it, I am a different person. I now create more content, tell more stories, write books etc. So, this time watching it, I was able to pick up a lot more things I didn't notice before.

Seeing the main character gradually transform into a monster made the show a masterpiece.

There are so many shows like this.

'Do I have to pull out a pencil and take notes?'
Nah, you don't need to turn this into a homework assignment.

The only rule is to watch without your phone present.

If you are watching one of these shows and hopping on your cell phone, then you have failed, my friend.

I'm guilty of this. I watched shows with my phone present and minor distractions prevented me from leveling up my storytelling skills.

Watch without your phone or put it on airplane mode.

'What about fictions books, Armani?'
With fiction books, you are doing active consumption.

I'd challenge you to read science fiction books.

Like:
- o   Dune
- o   Harry Potter
- o   Lord of the Rings

When you read science fiction books, your brain is being **forced** to turn words into out of world imagery. This stretches the thought waves and allows you to expand your storytelling skills as well.

Reading is different from watching because with watching, the imagery is presented to you.

While with reading, your brain is forced to work.

Reading fiction is a great way to understand how words lead to creating imagery in the mind. It will help you develop a feel for how stories unfold and how to get a general understanding for plot building.

There is a famous filmmaker named Werner Herzog who says he watches roughly 3-5 films a year, but he reads a **lot.**

I found that very strange.
Why is a filmmaker reading so much?

I would think that a filmmaker would watch a lot and an author would read a lot.

Werner Herzog was adamant in his advice. He said that it's smart to keep reading because it makes you sharper and a better storyteller.

It's not just about telling stories all the time. It's also about making the time to study and get better by consuming as well.

The best combination is when we are in the habit of telling stories **and** consuming consistently.

This is what we call the best of both worlds.

Unpredictability

You ever had that moment when you tried to shut away problems only to find yourself inviting more problems in?

It's like there is a feature in nature that says: 'Whoa, what do you think you're doing? Are you really trying to avoid problems?'

Then abnormal problems find you.

There was a moment when I was working on a book in 2020. This was going to be a book about public speaking called the Speaking Wizard.

My goal was to lock myself in my apartment and do nothing but work on the book.

This was meant to be a good thing.

I noticed when I left my apartment, that's when a

lot of problems would occur.

o   I'd get stuck in traffic.
o   Someone would mess up my fast-food order.
o   A rude club member would take out their aggression on me & I'd think about clapping back.

Well, if I'm going to be by myself in this living facility for the next few days, then problems must immediately disappear.

On the contrary, the exact opposite happened.
'What happened?'
My sink broke.

I never knew a sink breaking was a thing. Probably because the sink routinely working was something that I took for granted.

By it breaking, I mean it was clogged.

I thought this was going to be a quick fix. But then again, I don't know anything about sinks.

That's when I decided the writing is going to have to take a backseat so I can fix the sink.

I begin hitting up random plumbers around my area. A lot of the people I hit up had awful customer service.

I was hitting up the independent contractors because I wanted to get a deal.

But these independent contractors were too lackadaisical & some were flat out rude. Saying they couldn't be at my apartment for at least a week. Others were telling me to buy the parts, so it'll make their job easier.

Ha!
I'm hiring you to do the job. Not so I can participate with you, clown.

After hitting up a bunch of independent plumbers and leaving disappointed, I decided to hit up the corporations. They sent a member to my house who did an evaluation.

The plumber tells me:
'Geez, this is worse than I thought. I'm going to have to do a diagnosis first. I have no clue what's going on with the sink.'

'Um what do you think it's going to cost me?' I asked.
'My estimation is $400 or so,' he says.

400 dollars??
What the fuck.

'Okay, let me get back to you.'

That entire day was spent trying to solve this plumbing issue.

That's when one of my buddies hit me up and wanted to hang out. I told him I couldn't because I needed to save money to deal with this clogged sink.

He responded with:
'Clogged sink? Don't hire any of these idiots. I'm on my way.'

That's when he came to my place with a plunger. He puts the plunger in the sink, does 2 of the suction motions & then BOOM.

The sink suddenly drains…

That day, I learned when you try to avoid problems, you end up inviting more problems in.

Another lesson I learned is that problems often lead to entertaining stories in the future.

Unpredictability is bad when you don't have the storyteller's mindset. But when you do have a storyteller's mindset, unpredictability serves as a vehicle to draw more creative insights from.

E.A.R Formula

There will be plenty of times when you have a lot of things to say, but for some reason, the ideas aren't coming out.

This is when it's handy to have a few formulas that you can fall back on for inspiration.

Here's a formula that you can use for endless storytelling content.

E.A.R:
- o Embarrassing
- o Anxiety
- o Rock bottom

Let's go through each one.

Embarrassing

What are comedians really? They are funny story-tellers.

And what are they talking about a lot of the time? They are talking about a moment when they embarrassed themselves.

Most of the funniest stories were from past embarrassments.
- o   Healed pain = wisdom
- o   Healed embarrassment = humor

Think about a few moments that you found embarrassing.

Then tell a story of the embarrassing moment with the intention of making someone laugh. Laughter comes down to intention. It doesn't really matter what you say a lot of the times. If you make it the intent to make someone laugh, then your voice will change and become warmer.

Anxiety

Another place to get great storytelling material is from anxiety.

There was a speech in Toastmasters that I did called, F.E.A.R.

The premise of that talk was to share how I was afraid and anxious towards swimming.

When I was young, there was a little kid who

pushed me into the 6-foot side of the water.

As I was trying to keep myself from drowning, everyone was clapping because they thought I was swimming. When I would scream for help, water kept getting in my mouth.

Eventually, one of the aunties in the party was like:
'Oh my God, Arman is drowning!'

That's when my dad and a few people jumped into the water to save me. After that moment, I had anxiety towards swimming.

The F.E.A.R story went onto talk about my journey towards overcoming that anxiety. How the initial encounter with swimming eventually led me to learn swimming.

The journey was the reward.

At the end of the story, I realized that conquering the anxiety of swimming was great. But the deeper lesson was the illusion of fear.

F.E.A.R:
   o   False Evidence Appearing Real
   o   Face Everything and Rise

After the speech, I had a bunch of the crowd

members come up to me and say:
'Yo man, I have the same fear with dogs. I got chased by a dog when I was little, and it did a number on me. Your speech showed me that it's not too late to overcome a fear.'

The anxiety turned into hope and the hope turned into insights for the audience.

If you're in a leadership position, you don't always have to talk about how you are the *man*.

Instead, you should bring awareness to your flaws and show you rose above anyways.

Rock bottom

The rock bottom moment is when someone feels like their back is against the wall.

The rock-bottom moment can happen from:

- o   Losing a loved one
- o   Getting fired
- o   Getting dumped

Something.

This is another conflict that you are facing. The question is, how will you rise?

The rock bottom moment is the modern-day hero's journey.

The hero's journey is when the main character needs to prove themselves after being presented with a grand challenge.

What better way to communicate the hero's journey than to truly experience it?

I'm sure when you think about it, you've had a few of these moments that you can talk about.

That's the E.A.R formula.

Whenever your back is against the wall with content creation, these 3 letters of the acronym will save you.

Building Relatable Characters

Building relatable characters come down to being a great observer.

I want you to picture a dragon with social anxiety.

This may seem comical, until in your mind, you picture this dragon.

I'm picturing a green dragon who is fidgety with his movements. Even though he is a fire breathing dragon who should have the utmost confidence, you can tell from his jittery movements that he doesn't have self-esteem.

What does this imply?

It implies that when we are assessing relatable characters, we are assessing **human** experiences & emotions first.

I know damn well a dragon cannot exist. Especially one with social anxiety.

But when I combine a mythical animal with real human emotions, that's when the mythical animal becomes real.

You can do that with virtually any character out there.

The best part?
Inspiration is all around you.
Literally, it's all around you.

You should think about the characters in your life who are out of world personalities. Out of world personalities do not always imply something good. A lot of times, it implies something bad.

For example:
I know this guy who I'll call TJ.

TJ is one of the most socially intelligent people I have ever met. He can get along with people with ease.

He'll build inside jokes with others, hype them

up and tell stories with no difficulty. TJ has a lot of friends and a lot of acquaintances.

TJ's only problem?
He is a snake.

This man uses his charm to extract information from others and often uses it against them.

More specifically, he'll get information from his guy friends and gossip to his girl friends about it.

Despite him backstabbing so many people, others continue to give him a chance because he is such a great listener.

Why would people give someone who back-stabbed them another chance?

Do these people want to be heard that bad?

Yes, they do.

TJ teaches a few lessons about real human experience:
1.   A lot of socially intelligent people are sinister.
2.   Beware of who you vent to.
3.   Making someone feel heard is a superpower.

By the way, this is a real-world character who I know. All I did was switch up his name for plausible deniability.

If the real person came up to me and was like:
'Armani, are you talking about me when you say TJ?'

I can easily be like:
'Of course not! I'm talking about TJ. He is completely made up.'
wink-wink

The cheatcode to building relatable characters is looking at the characters in your own life and slapping different names on these individuals.

Remember, we are telling stories that are congruent to us. View yourself as the builder of Lego buildings.

When we take fragments of other people's personalities and combine our personalities, we build something entirely new!

The character of TJ had the snake moves. But did I mention that he used to be fat?

When he was fat, he was socially awkward. Him

What does this do?

Well, that made him more lethal in social skills.

The real-life version of TJ was always in shape. However, I added a different dimension of him being fat to give him more uniqueness. This is optional by the way.

What I'm trying to stress is that building relatable characters can be pretty fun. A lot of times, it can serve as a venting session. You are **finally** putting words to things you have noticed.

Relatable characters who you know are eerily similar to relatable characters in the most fantastic of tales...

The Silent Connection

Humans are different in many ways.
Humans are similar in many ways.

You can tell one of the most outlandish stories out there, and I guarantee there will be **at least** 1 person on the planet who is going to say:
'I feel like you are talking right to me.'

If there is at least 1 person like that, then there are at least 100 people like that. This shows that humans are much more connected than we initially gave ourselves credit for.

Beware though.

We don't want to tell stories with the intent of:

'How can I get this other person to connect with me?'

Instead, we want to tell stories with the intent of: 'I'll be authentic to who I am, and I'll expect at least 1 person to connect with me.'

o   Lead with yourself first.

This is very different than traditional approaches to content creation. Most people create content with the product mentality.

They do market research to see what others want to hear. That will work for some time, but eventually, the creator will burn out.

It's smart to give practical tips that work for you.

Want to create effortless content?
o   **Then give advice to your younger self.**

Some call it, *flow.*
Some call it, *getting in the zone.*
Some call it, *feeling the rhythm.*

All those imply the same thing:
o   Collapsing time.

That's when past, present and future seize to exist. When everything exists at once, you unlock masterful systems thinking.

Make a mockery out of time.

o   You can do this when you give advice to your younger self.

When you give advice to your younger self:
o   Present is going to the past.
o   Past is getting a message from the future.
Time becomes blurry.

When time becomes blurry, story mode is activated.

It's sort of like watching a YouTube video. Do see the time bar?
'Yeah.'

You can scroll along the time bar as you wish. In terms of you watching the video, time is a joke.

There are a lot of people who watch their content at 2x the speed. Time is becoming a laughingstock!

Another thing that happens when you make content for your younger self is that your personality shows.

Imagine if you were talking to your boss's, boss's, boss. How would you feel?
'I'd feel pretty stiff.'
Why?

'It's because this person has so much authority over me.'
Exactly.

Now imagine if you were talking to your 5-year-old cousin. How would you feel?
'I'd feel looser & more confident.'
Why?
'Because I am of the higher authority.'
Correct.

When you give advice to your younger self, you take the position of power & feel more confident. This is when insights come to you on autopilot.

You become the person viewing your life and adjusting the time bar at will.

Building Relatable Characters

Give advice to your younger self about something.
'About what?'
Anything.

If you have no clue where to look, look at your regrets. Or pick something that you know now that you wished you knew back then.

Picture it's just you and your younger self having a conversation.

This can be done in writing or speaking format.

Contagious Attitude

You ever seen someone who had so much belief in what they were saying that it seemed real?

The conviction in their voice was so strong that you began thinking:
Why would this person lie??

Some people lie due to fear. They are afraid of telling the truth because of the fear of being punished.

Other people lie because they actually think they are telling the truth.

This is when the other person thinks you're the one lying. Maybe there is some miscommunication going on or there is the wrong interpretation of the data.

Other times, a person lies due to a sinister reason. This is who I call the, *Pinocchio*. They are aware they are lying, but they do it anyways.

'Why do they lie like this, Armani?'
To create drama.

On Google, drama is defined as:
'An exciting, emotional, or unexpected series of events or set of circumstances.'

These people lie to get some drama going in their life. Maybe they are bored, who knows.

What makes someone else believe this lie?

It comes down to the enthusiasm they share this lie with.

The person shares this lie with so much enthusiasm and belief that eventually, the other person thinks:
'Geez, they must be onto something that I'm not.'

Enthusiasm is not built from only having a lot of energy.

Instead, it's built from having an attitude of knowing something that someone else doesn't.

Let's say I put you in a room with a few others to see who can find a box of money, otherwise, the room will explode.

But before I put you in the room, I tell you the exact location of where the money is and how the room is not going to explode. We are just filming a TV show and the goal is to get a reaction out of the other participants.

So, you are placed with 6 other panicking individuals.

Yet, you have this calm composure to you because you are perfectly aware of some information they are not.

This leads to enthusiasm from your end.

The enthusiasm is what becomes contagious.

'Armani, are you telling me to lie?'
No, I'm telling you to understand liars.

Understand liars and you'll understand a lot of storytelling.
   o   When was the last time you lied?
   o   When was the last time someone lied to you?

Analyze those experiences.

This analysis will teach you more about storytelling than you can possibly imagine.

Is Gossiping Primal?

There was this one time I got called in for a P1 at work. A P1 is short for priority 1 which meant the system was in critical condition.

What was supposed to be a regular workday turned into a workday from hell.

I worked without breaks, got yelled at on the phone and stared at the computer for hours trying to solve problems

By the time I was finally out, I just wanted to relax.

The highway was empty since I got out so late. I put on some music, followed the speed limit, and cruised.

Suddenly, there was this car that started aggressively tailgating me.

I looked around the road and saw the other lanes were empty. Why are you tailgating me for, bum?

If this car thought I was going to move out of his way, then he had another thing coming. This car will have to take an alternate lane, not me.

After 4 minutes of tailgating me, that's when the car went to the next lane and aggressively cut me off.

He cut me off so aggressively that he almost bumped into me.

I was livid.

I was already having a bad day and this idiot was going out of his way to make it worse.

That's when my primal side kicked in and I realized it was the perfect time to tailgate him. Let's give him a taste of his own medicine.

Right as I was about to tailgate him, I recalled that this highway had a lot of undercover cops who were itching to give drivers a ticket.

Due to the risk, I decided to hold out.

My blood was boiling, and I was feeling a lot of physical sensations for taking the high road.

By the time I finally got home, I clearly had an upset face. My roommate asked me what was up. That's when something magical happened.

I went into storytelling mode.

'Bro, you won't believe it. I was having a long day at work. The systems crashed.... I spent hours working on it. When I got out, there was this thug who began tailgating me and trying to get me in a car accident...'

I was telling this compelling story without ANY planning beforehand.

The mean tailgater was automatically being amplified with depth and personality traits. The setting was designed. The plot was unfolding.

This showed me that storytelling is who we are: **It's primal.**

We often just need to move out of our own way.

Not only is storytelling primal, so is gossiping.

There are 5 human desires:
  o   Desire to know.

o   Desire to bond.
o   Desire to feel.
o   Desire to protect.
o   Desire to acquire.

If you look closely, gossiping appeals to desire to *know* and *feel*.

It doesn't matter if you gossip or not, just notice others who are gossiping.

They physically FEEL good when they are sharing & receiving information about others.

Gossipping implies that humans are natural born storytellers. I doubt they took courses on how to develop this trait. It is a primal way to communicate information.

I'm pretty sure our ancient ancestors were gossiping somehow. Maybe with cave art, hand gestures, grunts etc. This is why so many people gossip without any conscious effort.

Puppet Master

In this world, there are 2 types of people:
- o   Puppets.
- o   Puppet masters.

When I bring up the phrase, puppet master, what do you think?
'Someone who is very sinister.'

What about if I bring up the phrase to a little kid. How do you think they will perceive, puppet master?
'As entertainment.'

The meaning of puppet master is subjective. For the time being, we need to put our negative interpretations of the phrase aside.

A true storyteller is a puppet master.

We need to understand that there are pure story

tellers & evil ones.

There are groups of people who spread division, hate & fearmonger.

Why?
Because they want to create a drama.

Control someone's heart & it's easy to control their mind.

That's what happens with content in general.

You'll see a lot of people who create stories do so with the intention of getting more ratings and clicks. These are the type of people who are telling stories without any set principles. They control hearts and minds, but not in a good way. This is not the type of content that has the consumer feeling 20 inches taller after consuming it.
   o   Instead, they feel oppressed & fearful.

There are other storytellers who have a purpose. Ratings, views, and money are the byproducts. What is the purpose?? That's king!

The day the purpose is forgotten is the day that havoc ensues:
   o   There is no longer a theme to the mind. There is no longer a theme to the content.

o   Everything is scattered without unity.

Just like there are puppets and puppet masters, there are creators and consumers.

A top tier storyteller is a mix of a creator and a consumer.

Just know the messages that you put out there is altering how someone views life and will alter their behaviors.

Therefore, understand how the game works.

All puppet masters are not bad.
It comes down to the intent.

Pursue Purpose
& Strategic Curiosity

The word 'purpose' often leads the mind to think something grand or big. That's faulty thinking.

Purpose does not have to have to be big (although, it can).

What matters more is the effect the behavior is having on the entire system.

There was one day when I was about to record a video called, *the Power of the Smile,* for my You-Tube channel. This video was going to discuss how smiling helps reduce speech anxiety.

As I'm about to record the video, I noticed something.
The screw on top of the camera stand was missing. Without the screw, I am unable to connect

the camera to the camera stand.

If I just rest the camera on the camera stand, then it will slide off and shatter. Did I mention this is a 700-dollar camera??

Okay, well I can't record the video until the screw is found.

What was supposed to be a 10-minute video suddenly turned into a 1.5-hour man hut. I mean 'screw hunt.'

After the 1.5 hours, I came out empty handed.

What now?

Sure, I could record the video on my phone, but that would not solve the issue. I had more videos to record for the week.

I will go to Best Buy (that's where I bought the camera) & get a screw from there.

Soon as I got to Best Buy, I'm greeted by 2 goobers. One big black guy, and one little white guy. They were both aggressively trying to sell me a camera.

After some time passes, I tell them my camera is working fine, all I need is a tiny screw.

'Just the screw??' they asked in amazement.
'Just the screw,' I said.

'Well, we don't have JUST the screw, sir. You're going to have to buy the entire camera stand.'
'How much?' I ask.

'70 dollars,' they say.

70 dollars for just the screw? No way. I had just bought a laptop a few weeks earlier and didn't have the funds to spend so much money on something so tiny.

Another 1.5 hours wasted at Best Buy.

I decided to come back home and continue the search.

By the time I came home, I see something shiny under the table.

You ever had that moment when you dropped something, and it ended up super far away from where you dropped it? Well, that's what happened to me.

The screw was under a table far away from the YouTube studio.

That's when I:

1. Plugged the screw on the camera stand.
2. Put the camera on the camera stand.
3. Recorded the video.
4. Uploaded the video on YouTube.
5. The video was watched by 100+ people.
6. 5 of the 100 people told me they applied the tip.
7. 1 of the 5 messaged how they did the smile trick, cooled off their nerves & gave a stellar speech to a group of 40 people.

Who knows how many of the 40 people will apply the tips from the speech & pay it forward?

This all would not have been possible without a tiny screw.

Don't you see?

In terms of the system, it's not the physical size that is king.

It's the meaning that is king.

When we pursue purpose, we should disengage: 'What's in it for me?' thinking.

And engage: 'What's in it for the system?' thinking.

That's true purpose.

That's what allows a tiny screw to turn into the missing puzzle piece for something much grander.

People who pursue purpose, build.
It doesn't matter what exactly they build, but they need to build something.

It can be building a:
  o   Business.
  o   Physique.
  o   Family.
  o   Content.
Etc.

Once building mode is activated, that's when strategic curiosity is activated.

'What's the difference between strategic curiosity and regular curiosity?'
The difference is direction.

Let's say Stacy was not building anything. Her mind would still get curious because that's how the mind is programmed. The only problem is that there is no theme to her curiosities.

One day, she is getting curious about gossip. The next day, she is getting curious about calculus. Another day, she is getting curious about political

Scandals.

She's all over the place.

Let's say her twin sister, Sable, is **building** a fashion brand.

Her goal is to sell lipstick, makeup tutorials, books and much more.

Now she is at the stage of building systems for her business. Sable will get curious with a theme.

Her theme is:
  o   How can she continue to keep her fashion brand growing and profitable?

Her curiosity will take her on a mental journey.

The only difference between Sable and her sister is that Sable is pursuing purpose. By pursuing purpose, Sable's curiosities have a direction.

From the outside, it looks like disorder.
From the inside, elegant learning is unfolding in real time.

.

Be Human

What separates storytelling from other forms of content is that it rewards being relatable.

The more relatable you are, the better your content will be. You don't have to pretend to be someone you're not.

Here's a mental hack:
o   Get your name and add 'Talks' at the end.

Earlier, I said that you can create an alternate nickname to help you get in the storytelling zone.

An example is:
o   Your name is Matt.
o   Your nickname is Matty.
o   Therefore, the final output will be **Matty Talks.**

This hack makes it easier to express your ideas.

Which subjects resonate with you?

A great storyteller looks IN first then then looks OUT.

In the process of looking in is where riveting content is found.

Storytellers turn:
  o   Data into information.
  o   Then deliver the information with personality.

Whatever your personality is, rock it. If you're a private guy, then articulate the experiences of a private guy who is aiming to say a lot while saying little.

If you're a sarcastic guy, then tell the stories of being misunderstood for being sarcastic.

If you're a past asshole turned kind, then express life from your lens.

The more you understand yourself, the more you are capable of understanding others.

Storytelling is one of the few fields that rewards flaws.

Try being an aircraft pilot who messes up a lot. You'll get fired.

While with storytelling, the more you mess up, the more data you have which you can craft into information and turn that information into stories. This field is designed for you to succeed forever.

Learn the art of storytelling by understanding the good, bad, and ugly sides of you.

.

Emotional Tone Scale

In the Tampa Bay area, there is a Scientology church not too far away from me.

In 2019, one of my buddies told me that his mentor told him to check out the Scientology church and see what it was about. Apparently, this church gives a lot of practical tips on communication skills & mind management.

My friend asked me to join along.

Immediately, I shut it down. I heard a lot of negative news about Scientology & was not trying to have anything happen to me.

That's when my friend said:
'Okay, if you don't go, then I'm not going either.'

When he said that, I decided to reconsider my

position. At that stage, I realized I was generalizing Scientology.

I didn't know anything about this field.
I saw a South Park episode on it & heard some people mentioning it on the Joe Rogan podcast.

o   If they are not that bad, I learned something new.
o   If they are bad, then I have a funny story to tell.

I told my buddy, *fine,* I'll go with him to check it out.

By the time I went, I was greeted by a few attractive women who gave us a tour.

In the tour, we were given insight into the history of Scientology, book recommendations and watched some course videos.

One of the videos which stuck out was the one on the Emotional Tone Scale. I really enjoyed that video because it broke down emotions to a science.

The scale showed the different range of emotions all humans experience. When I saw this scale, it reminded me of the electromagnetic spectrum.

Long story short, I didn't go back to the Scientology church again. Nothing against them, it just wasn't for me.

But what I did leave away with was an insight into the emotional tone scale.

The scale organizes the series of emotions from the most empowering to the most draining. They are:
- o Love
- o Enthusiasm
- o Fun
- o Boredom
- o Antagonism
- o Anger
- o Fear

Scientology used the emotional tone scale more for leadership and vocal coaching.

What I got out of the emotional tone scale was how it was an adjustable dial for a storyteller to control someone's internal world.

Emotional intelligence, content creation and storytelling are all joined at the hip. There is no separating them.

When the entire emotional tone scale is embraced, that's when life becomes one large drama, story & play.

Think about it.

If you're someone who can use the **entire** emotional tone scale and harness it towards creativity, you transcend duality.

You're no longer just:
- o Happy when good things happen.
- o Sad when bad things happen.

Instead, everything good and bad is a part of the emotional tone scale that adds color to your story.

What is the meaning of gratitude?

The wrong definition will cause you to practice incorrectly.

If someone tells you:
'Gratitude is only when you count your big wins.'

Then there is a chance that you will be only looking for your big wins, like:
- o Getting a job promotion.
- o Closing a big client.
- o Getting a new car.

What about the small wins?

You may grow a disdain towards small wins if you only count the big wins. A small win is perceived as a loss or flat out ignored.

MUCH BETTER TO FLIP IT.

o   When you count the small wins, then counting the big wins happen on autopilot.

You know what's even more advanced?
When you see the wisdom in the wins and losses.

When you see the wisdom in the wins and losses, that's when you are becoming a genius storyteller & boosting maturity.

When you see wisdom in the wins and losses, that's when you are activating the **entire** emotional tone scale.

It doesn't matter which emotion it is, the storyteller will find a way to use it towards their favor.

It's because a storyteller is resourceful.

"I did so much with so little that I can do anything with something."

Pattern Interrupts

There are sometimes when patterns are needed. This allows us to extract meaning efficiently. Especially for logical fields.

Other items, we need to introduce pattern interrupts.

When you are a storyteller who is looking for authentic ideas, that's when you become better with spotting creativity and thriving under moments of chaos.

Interrupt the patterns purposefully to become more creative.

There are a few mental hacks to get the most out of pattern interrupts if you find yourself in a rut.

Messy Living Facility

I'm sure you've heard the advice of changing up your living facility.

If you normally write indoors, then go outdoors. If you normally write in your apartment, then go to a hotel lobby.

Another thing that I will recommend is the messy trick.

'The messy trick?'
Yes, allow your place to be a bit messy.

Not too messy to a point where it's disgusting, and flies are roaming around.

But getting some clothes and leaving them in the living room doesn't hurt.

'Why would I possibly want to be messy? Especially in my living facility of all places?'
The main reason why is because this activates chaos in you.

o   Creativity = Structured chaos.

When you have chaos, it's easier to structure it. When you have nothing, then nothing can be structured.

When your external environment is messy,

the thought waves are less tamed.

'Less tamed?? Geez, that seems scary!'

At first, maybe. But you can also view it as a mental adventure.

This is just an idea.

Opposite Hand Trick

Another idea is to write with your opposite hand.

o   If you're normally right-handed, switch it up.
o   If you're normally left-handed, you know the drill.

The reason that this works is because your body influences the mind. When the body is being forced into a new mode of movement, it alters the mind. This allows for new thought waves.

Unorthodox thought waves guide a storyteller towards greatness.

Think this:
'I will make 100,000 dollars.'

Making 6 figures is nothing to scoff at. In many places, it's the top 1%.

Now alter that with:
'I will give a trillionaire dollars worth of value.'

Do you feel that?

The thought waves generated by the second statement led to more feelings in your body.

A storyteller's mind should be absorbed in big thoughts. There is a physical equivalent to this.

You ever seen those muscular guys who couldn't touch their toes? They were so big but lacked any semblance of flexibility.

Who is to say some flexibility wouldn't help them lift more?

With creativity, our aim is to have a flexible mind.

You can think unpredictable thoughts in many ways. Swapping your writing hand is just one of many methods.

If you rarely use a pencil, then alternate the mouse on your laptop.

Not only does this exercise boost creativity, but it also helps with anger issues. You'll feel calm and relaxed.

Poster trick

There are 2 possible options for using posters to think big.
- o   Image of the universe.
- o   Image of fire.

I leverage both.

If you've ever watched me on YouTube, you'll notice that there is a big fire & mic poster that rests behind me.

'What's the big deal about fire?'
At first, I thought the same thing.

For some reason, fire made me feel a certain type of way and I couldn't explain why.

One day, I ran into 2 monks outside of Dunkin Donuts. How often do you run into monks??

I noticed they were holding onto laptops.

Whoa, monks were allowed laptops? I guess I was very ignorant on this lifestyle.

I asked them:
'Why are your robes orange?'

They said the robes were orange because orange symbolizes fire. Fire represents knowledge & the dispelling of darkness.

- o   Knowledge = Fire
- o   Ignorance = Darkness

That's when it began to make so much sense.

A storyteller tells truth. To tell truth, you need to express knowledge. Knowledge is represented by fire. That's why fire was resonating so much with me.

I believe there is something **primal** about fire.

Don't believe me?
Stare at FIRE.

It can be a YouTube video, or you can light up a candle. Do you feel that?
'Whoa…. I do, what is that?'
It's a pattern interrupt. There is something in us that is primal and beyond the expression of words alone. Fire connects us with that primal side.

Therefore, leverage the fire poster and see if it helps boost your creativity.

Universe Poster

Another poster that you can get is of the Universe.

'Why the poster of the universe?'
The reason why is because intellect is a tool that we use in the domain of Earth.

It comes in handy and allows us to create plenty of useful formulas. But the universe is larger than Earth, duh.

The Earth is a subset of the universe.
The universe is the superset.

When we stare at the picture of the universe, we bypass logic. We engage superset thinking.

What do creative people often say?
    o   'I get my best creative ideas when I'm not thinking too much and being too logical.'

The poster of the universe is a hack for creative thinking.

Don't take my word for it, try it out for yourself.

Give yourself an innovative prompt to tell a story about. Preferably something that you find difficult.

If you don't have one, here's a fun one to play

around with:
'Why is it socially acceptable to have dogs as pets, but not squirrels? Talk about this in a story format designed to make me inquire and laugh.'

That's when you may be like:
'I don't know if I can do that.'

Stare at the universe poster.
Now write.

Napkin Hack and Exercise

Sometimes, the outline will hold you back. Planning too much kills creativity.

Creativity is born from a lack of planning.

Other times, the outline will help you out and give direction.

Different people have different creative processes. What I want you to tryout is the napkin trick.

1. Get a napkin.
2. Crumple it up.
3. Then write an outline for a story on that.

'Wait a minute, Armani. So many questions. Number 1, why a napkin and not a notebook? Number 2, why crumple it up?'

The reason we are choosing a napkin is because

it is more informal. Being too formal causes us to be too logical which kills our creative juices.

Instead, the napkin is informal and bypasses over-thinking.

The smaller your napkin, the more creative you become.

If your napkin is large, then fold it.

As for your second question, why crumple it up?

The main reason is because we are turning:
   o   An already informal act into an even more informal one.

This allows us to really get our creative juices flowing.

'Anything else?'
Use a timer.

A timer counting down raises the stakes and builds creativity & efficiency.

'Anything else??'
Create a dire situation for yourself.

If you don't get the outline complete in 29

seconds, then you will be shot in the head.

How much you believe this narrative will dictate how creative you become.

Recap:
1. Find a writing prompt.
2. Get a napkin.
3. Crumple up the napkin.
4. Set a timer.
5. Create a scary narrative if you don't get the outline complete.
6. Start creating the outline.

Practice it till you Become It

Stories define who we are.
There are different ways that we are going to be practicing.

Each person who reads this book will use the knowledge in different ways.

o   Some people will use it to overcome their analysis paralysis with content creation.
o   Others will double down on their YouTube channel.
o   Others will stop taking themselves so seriously in social interactions and be perfectly fine with rejection.
o   Others will use stories to inspire their employees rather than putting them to sleep.

Whatever we do, we need to practice.

The last thing you want to be is an armchair storyteller. The one who sits on their ass and is like:
'If it were me, I would have done that.'

Then do it.

Storytelling is one of the few fields where you get
better with time. It is a mental sport that you can
play for the rest of your life.

I don't want to give you an exact storytelling practice procedure because it's a creative process.
Here's my routine though:
- o   I write an email every day.
- o   I write daily tweets.
- o   3 short YouTube videos a week.
- o   3 short podcast episodes a week.
- o   3 blogs a week.

But that's just me.
You can copy routines.
But avoid copying rituals.

'What's the difference?'
- o   Rituals = Routines + Narrative

At first, it's cool to borrow other people's
routines because you have no clue what to do.

There are writers who just journal every day, and
that's about it for their storytelling practice.

There are speakers who wake up every morning and talk out loud to themselves to get their day started.

It doesn't have to be some grand spectacle of a routine.

With storytelling, you know you are practicing **incorrectly** when you think you're on the verge of figuring it out.

This is an infinite field.

After one story has been crafted, you should feel capable of crafting 50 more if needed. That's what we are practicing towards.

Eventually, you'll develop your own routine with your twist to it. That's when the routine blossoms into a ritual.

It's slowly becoming a part of you.

You know one thing I'm surprised more people are not fascinated by?
'What's that?'
Subconscious acts.

Like driving.

Isn't it dope that we can drive so seamlessly with

out thinking? Heck, when we think, we throw off our rhythm.

Same with typing.
I'm not thinking about exactly where I am going to be putting the fingers for the letters to appear. It just happens at this point.

Another one that surprised me was the Rubik's cube.

I learned how to solve a Rubik's cube because others thought I wasn't smart enough to solve it.

You don't need much intelligence to solve one. There are a bunch of tutorials on it.

After going through those tutorials, I probably solved the Rubik's cube 2,000+ times.

After some time, I lost my Rubik's cube. I didn't see it for years.

One day, I went to a friend's party, and he had a Rubik's cube.

I picked it up and started playing with it.

That's when he asked:
'Can you solve that? I've been trying to solve this for so long but haven't been able to.'

I smiled and said:
'I used to be able to solve it.'

He gave me a look like I was lying.

So, I used my intellectual effort to try to solve it.
I was putting so much thought into each move,
yet I was falling flat. What was going on?

I used to solve it so easily before. Now
my superpowers had faded.

That's when I was getting fed up.
I sat down on a nearby chair in frustration with
the Rubik's cube toggling between my palms.

That's when I started to relax.

It was at that point my fingers began to move on
its own & I felt like an observer going for a ride.

The Rubik's cube was getting closer & closer to
getting solved.

After 2 minutes and 29 seconds, the Rubik's cube
was solved. I rushed to my friend and showed
him.

He looked at me in shock.

He messed it up again and told me to solve it in

front of him.

This time, I used little conscious effort & focused on relaxing.

Once again, the Rubik's cube was solved. This is when my friend went around the party to announce what I just did.

'Yo, Armani can solve a Rubik's cube!'

I looked at my palms & noticed something miraculous.

Normally, I took driving cars for granted.
I took brushing my teeth for granted.
I took typing for granted.

It was at that moment with the Rubik's cube when I finally understood what a 'habit' was.
   o   Habit building = Automating a human.

How dope is that?!

I'm practicing so I can automate myself and surprise myself in each practice session.

You can do that with storytelling. **Practice so consistently that you become it.**

Eventually, you don't need to think on how to tell

a story. Later in the game, most of your focus will be on how to relax.

This is amazing, my friend.

You really are rewiring yourself on a being level at this point.

Content Creation HACK

I'm going to give you a revolutionary formula that will change your life if you apply it.

This is beyond storytelling by the way.
Yes, it will help you tremendously in your story-telling journey, but it's more than that.

It will alter your perception.

Before I give you the hack, I need to give you some context.

Currently, big data and artificial intelligence are 2 of the biggest concepts bought up in the tech field.

Big data is when companies have a lot of data due to the advancement of information technology.

Artificial intelligence is machine learning on

crack. It's when decision making is refined & polished so machines can do work that humans find complex or tedious.

Well, big data and machine learning have a symbiotic relationship.

'What does that mean?'
It means the 2 benefit each other.

Artificial intelligence becomes more refined with the more data it gets.

And big data is incapable of being processed by traditional computers. It needs advanced infrastructure like the tools used for artificial intelligence.

The more the 2 work together, the more both parties win.

   o   Big data gets processed.
   o   Artificial intelligence has refined movements.

Likewise, we can do the same with ourselves and our content.
Let's say you record YouTube videos.

More specifically, you create a private YouTube channel on the side.

(Yes, private YouTube channels are possible. I'm surprised how many people are completely unaware of this concept. All you have to do is not make the video public. More people should have private YouTube channels and watch their growth in real time!!)

You end up creating talks on topics that interest you and resonate with your big purpose. 3 videos a week.

Over 6 months, you have a wide range of videos.

As you are recording these videos, watch them back.

Watching back your videos does a few things:

1.   You are watching a video of yourself which allows you to collapse subject/object duality. You identify as pure awareness.
2.   Brain thinks new thought waves. Normally, you perceive life through 1st person perspective. But when your brain is watching a video yourself, it opens a new perspective to reality! You'll feel light buzzing sensations in your brain that indicates physiological changes. This is you using information systems to rewire the nervous system.
3.   You're collecting more data to spot what you are doing well & which moves to cut back on.

The more data you have, the better.

Every morning, I watch 1 video, listen to 1 podcast, and read 1 blog.

Since we are doing the YouTube route, let's talk about how I consume videos.

I'll watch videos from up to 2019. Boy, was I awful! My delivery back then makes me cringe. All good.

Machine learning and big data learns best when it has a variety of data in its arsenal. If all the data is similar, then the chances of reaching stunning insights reduces.
The more data you have (ranging from old content to new content) the more refined your movements will be.

So, spend time consuming 1 video of yourself a day.

Overtime, your brain will start to think new thoughts. It will be easier to visualize yourself with clarity.

More importantly, you will develop a feel for storytelling.

You ever heard of Tom Brady, the quarterback?

'Yeah. He's regarded as the greatest quarterback of all time.'
Yep, that one.

Watch his Facebook documentary called, *Tom Against Time*.

Normally, he is a private guy. But in this documentary, he gives a look into what it takes to become a top performer. In the documentary, it shows how serious Tom is about watching game film.

He doesn't only watch recent games. He watches his first season games as well. The more data he has, the better his decision making gets.

Being a quarterback has physical elements to it, but it is mainly a mental sport.

Same thing with storytelling.

You don't only have to do videos by the way. The content trick works for podcasts and blogs too.
- o   Big data = Stories
- o   Artificial intelligence = Nervous System

Fearlessness

The last section covers one of the most important character traits to be a great storyteller: *Fearlessness.*

'Armani, you already talked about how to handle rejection. Isn't that like fearlessness?'
Not quite.

Becoming fearless is a learned trait. A person becomes fearless through the vehicle of storytelling.

Since storytelling is discovering truth, the person who makes truth the priority eventually learns how to let go of control.

When you try to control things too much, that's when you take the fun out of storytelling.

Fun and storytelling go hand in hand.
Fun and fearlessness go hand in hand.

When Stephen King was asked about his storytelling process, he said that it was like a discovery process.

He was learning where the story was going as much as the characters in the plot.

That's what wonderful storytellers eventually learn to do:
o   **They learn to allow things to flow.**

When flowing, it becomes much more fun. Throughout the process of storytelling, you eventually learn to view yourself as the instrument.

   o   Hard skills are about learning how to use instruments.
   o   Soft skills are about becoming the instrument.

The more you become the instrument, the more you take the spotlight off yourself.

The more you take the spotlight off yourself, the easier it becomes to deliver a compelling message.

So many people get excited when they hear no

2 thumbprints are the same. But no 2 anything is the same.

The more you allow yourself to become secondary to the truth, the more you allow yourself to view your experiences as the object.

Nowadays, data storytelling is becoming more of a thing.

Mainly because data is seen as the new oil. These large companies are capable of extracting meaning from the data that has been collected in the past of couple of years.

The main goal of that data is to make useful business decisions. Just collecting data for the sake of collecting it is not that useful.

But collecting data which will turn into insights that will help the business gain more money and/or reduce costs?
Sign me up.

It's same with storytelling. Rather than getting data from the business and past customers, we get data from our memories and our life.

One insight is all it takes to change your life forever.

Conclusion

Without understanding the fundamentals, you'll have 0 clue what is important and what is unimportant.

Fundamentally, storytelling is a string of ideas.

Stamp this definition in your mind and you'll be able to tell effortless stories overtime.

We are not in the game of learning theory and leaving it at that. The goal is to keep telling stories.

Instead of being a passive consumer, find ways to create your own path. This is the era where so many people can learn the art and science of storytelling.

o   Art thrives in chaos.

o   Science thrives with rules.
o   Storytelling thrives under both.

You want to know something that I always found crazy?
'What?'
Some of the best communicators started off shy and soft spoken.

This was apparent when I was a part of Toastmasters. I talked to the other members and learned so many of them started the club because they were shy.

Some of them took **years** to step foot into the club.

How random is it that these are the people who are a part of a public speaking club?

If you were to ask me, it's not that random.

Because behind your biggest pain lies the biggest opportunity for growth.

o   Some people may say they are 'not creative.'
o   Or not a 'natural born storyteller.'
o   Or there is not much emotion in their voice.

The excuses are limitless, I can guarantee you

that.

I come from a hard skills dominant field and the idea of an engineer learning storytelling back in my era (and I'm not even that old) was seen as laughable.

The only communication skills class we got was called 'communications for engineers.'

The main thing we learned in that class was how to tie a tie.

We never learned storytelling.
But guess what? I still learned it over time.

If a hard skills dominant guy like me can learn it, anyone can.

It's about reminding yourself of the fundamentals:
- o   Stories are a connection of ideas.
- o   Keep yourself secondary to the idea.
- o   Always pursue purpose, truth & practice.

That's all it takes to become a top 3% storyteller.

An idea that lies in the mind, dies in the mind.

An idea that is worth $3.48 in the mind is capable

of being worth $3,480 when articulated.

How many ideas like that do you have?

We'll never know until you tell those stories...bud.

The Information Age was a blast.

Now let's dominate the Storytelling Age....

Afterward

Thank you for making it to the end of the book!

If you enjoyed the book, I'd really appreciate if you could leave me a review on Amazon and let me know your honest thoughts.

This is the era where a revolution is happening. More people are going to learn how to communicate.

I believe this book will help people understand the basic elements of the art and science of storytelling.

Humans are information processing systems. One of the easiest ways to process information is through stories that are relatable and filled with at least 1 lesson.

The ArmaniTalks brand predominantly focuses on soft skills. The beauty is that all softs skills intertwine at one point or another.

Creativity enters the world of public speaking. Public speaking and storytelling go hand in hand. To control the nerves for the speech, emotional intelligence is needed. And for emotional intelligence, concentration is a must. If you can concentrate, then you can listen with ease. Listening is the staple of social skills.

All the soft skills were connected all along...

If you enjoyed this book, be sure to check out www.armanitalks.com. This website has my blogs, other books, YouTube videos, podcasts and much more!

Also, I run a free daily newsletter that teaches you how to articulate your ideas with clarity & confidence.
If you are interested, be sure to sign up on: https://armanitalks.com/newsletter/

Once again, thank you very for reading and I hope you level up your storytelling skills!!

Printed in Great Britain
by Amazon

77625081R00164